Early Praise

The **Wishing Shelf** loved this book so much we awarded it **5 STARS!**

All organizations, except some government sites, verified and approved their inclusion in this book. Here are some of their comments.

"Reading your writing is like yoga for the soul."
– Meg Jansen, Kids for Peace

"This book is a priceless collection of insights, ideas, tools and practical guidance on how each of us can create meaningful change—both in our own lives and for the greater good."
– Matthew Schwartz, Idealist.org

"I appreciate what you are doing to generously spread more resources, kindness, light and good energy. I especially love your *#43 Heal your wounds. Know you can.* and *#84 Release the (k)nots.*—within this fabulous book."
– Michael Reed Gach, Ph.D., Acupressure.com

"We are honored to be included in your book and especially love that you've acknowledged young people as a valuable part of our society. Just like *#65 See children as a gift*, this book is a gift and a guide for parents and peace-builders everywhere." – Kids for Peace

"A great collection filled with insights, tips, and resources to empower and inspire every journey."
– Jennifer Herrera, National Women's History Museum

101 Ways to Wow! Our World

Debbie Jenae

Inspired 101

About the cover: The daisy, a sunburst in flower form, reminds us of the love at our center with the potential to reach out in every direction, affecting our world—yours and ours—in the most positive ways. Daisies throughout the book provide additional reminders.

Copyright © 2025, 2013 by Deborah Jenae
All rights reserved.

First edition, published as *Be An Inspiration!* in 2013.
Second edition, *101 Ways to Wow! Our World,* 2025.

No part of this book may be reproduced or distributed in any form without written permission, except as permitted under copyright law for brief quotations embodied in articles and reviews.

For more information, contact
Inspired 101, P. O. Box 1054, Santa Ynez, CA 93460 USA
www.inspired101.com

ISBN 978-0-9889879-3-7 (soft cover)
ISBN 978-0-9889879-5-1 (hard cover)
ISBN 978-0-9889879-4-4 (e-book)

Library of Congress Control Number: 2024909139

No AI generated content was used in this book.
See back pages for illustration permissions and credits.
The country noted on each photograph reflects the location of the photographer or photo—a reminder of our connection to the world.

Mention of specific organizations in this book does not imply their endorsement.

While the author has made every effort to ensure the accuracy and completeness of information contained in this book at the time of publication, neither the author or publisher assumes any responsibility for errors or changes that occur after publication.

To *you,* for all you are.

Contents

The Book

Author's Note and a Promise	ix
How to use this book	xi
Introduction	xiii

The Author

The Inspiration	215
Q & A with Debbie	219
About Debbie	241

101 Ways to Wow!

2-page List	2
101 Ways defined	7
101 Ways by Category	
About Categories	149
Taking care of yourself	150
If you or someone you know needs help	153
Relating to children	154
In your community	157
Habits worth keeping	158
Things to think about	161

Reach Out

For Parents & Caregivers	165
About Reporting	166
Counseling	167

Resources

About Resources	173
CALL for Help, Support	174
FIND a Helping Resource	178
Arts	180
Continuing Education	182
Empowering Survivors	183
Equality, Partnership, Women	185
Healthy Mind, Body, Spirit	188
Legal	191
Parents & Caregivers	192
Peace-Building	194
Positive News / Inspiring Video	196
Volunteer	198
Youth	202
Phone Numbers	209
Websites	210

Credits & More

Acknowledgments	225
Bibliography	227
Further Reading	229
Illustration Credits	232
Index	235
Important Numbers	243

Author's Note and A Promise

I am delighted you've picked up this book!

Why? Forward movement. It means you're ready to feel more empowered. You're ready to stop buying into the fear that others are selling and redirect your energy to make a more positive difference in the world—yours and ours, it's all the same.

How? Fresh perspective, 101 ways, and lots of resources to help you refocus on living the life you want to experience by using your gifts to the best of your ability. As you explore these 101 ways, you may notice a need to clear some negative emotions, limiting beliefs, or old patterns. You'll get some insight on that, too. Meanwhile…

I *promise* to inspire you. I promise you some genuine WOW moments. And I promise you will look ahead with more understanding, acceptance, and optimism than ever before. So, let's get started!

Debbie Jende

How to use this book

- Read the *Introduction* to understand the intention of this edition, *The Inspiration* for the back story, and the *Q&A* for the changes and more insight.

- Take an estimated 2 minutes to read through the entire 2-page list of *101 Ways*. Be prepared for an innerwhelming[1] of loving energy.

- Flip through all the pages to get a feel for the content and message. Stop and read what catches your eye. Trust your intuition.

- Flag those that are relevant to you now, that you want to remember going forward, or that you want to pass on or apply to other relationships.

- Use the *Category* pages when you need a lift or for inspiration around a theme.

- Check the *Resources* for all organizations[2] mentioned in this book.

---

[1] By *innerwhelm* I mean to fill to overflowing with hope, joy, and optimism from a loving source that radiates from deep within. It's personal, internal, and deeply connecting.

[2] The few exceptions are footnoted.

Introduction

101 Ways to *Wow!* Our World. That's a pretty big idea, and it's intended to create a more loving world for everyone. How? By reminding you of your magnificence, your power to affect change, and the value you bring to the planet. Yikes! But hear me out because it gets way better!

The Good News

Old belief systems of power and control are breaking down, while our society becomes more heart-centered and holistic. The evidence is all around us: equal rights movements, self-help programs, alternative medicine, Earth care initiatives, good news sites, just to name a few. Within that evidence are the qualities of caring, inclusion, cooperation, and creativity that have been suppressed for ages yet are critical to our well-being and our survival. It's a rebalance of feminine and masculine energies that is long overdue. Yet the transition makes for challenging times, so we need to shift our attention from the negative to the results we want to achieve.

3 Challenges

As a society, we are aware of violence and oppression, and want to make it stop. So why isn't more being done? An **awareness/denial dynamic**. It feels too big, too scary. Where do you start? Even hearing or talking about it can quickly feel overwhelming. Why? Because it affects us all—victim, offender, enabler, witness, or bystander. So we tune out and turn away, not realizing that we don't have to have all the answers. Yet talking about it, understanding it, *and engaging positive actions* will encourage healing, stop the cycle, and move us forward.

Then there's the **archaic patriarchal domination mentality** that has to be seen for the destructive pattern it has become. Simply put, half the population cannot continue to be minimized, punished, and dismissed because they are female. It just doesn't make sense, except to those that are trying so desperately to keep control. And that desperation is affecting other populations as well as the historical record from which we learn—all deserving a fresh look from a much broader and inclusive perspective. Imagine the ideas, cures, achievements, inventions, and collaborations that have never been tried because those voices were silenced.

Which leads to a third challenge: **information overload.** It comes from a number of sources. It's not all good, it's not all true, and it's not all information. There's skepticism, cynicism, criticism and, if not a focus on bad news, negative bias has reached a critical level. While social and other media can be instrumental in positive change, the attention often settles on the mundane, the superficial, and petty competitiveness. It encourages users and viewers to obsess about what others are doing, rather than what they could be doing.

Common Element

All three challenges have one thing in common: **Fear.** Fear is a big incentive. It's used to make us worry, even obsess, about a lack of such things as peace, safety, money, health, and salvation to the point of paralysis. Fear mongers encourage doubt and anxiety to control our thoughts, purchases, votes, and decisions. Why? Profit and a misguided sense of power, with not a whole lot of thought about anyone's well-being. And the fear-mongers? They are afraid of losing what they have allowed to define them. But too much fear breeds negativity, disrespect, and violence as people feel more out of control of their own destinies and move further away from their own potential.

But here's the thing: If we're not mindful of these tactics, and keep all our attention on the aftermath or the possibility of trauma, harm, and disaster, very little goes to appreciation, discovery, collaboration, and opportunity. Worse yet, we start to see the world through their distorted lens and soon forget or deny all the good that's happening in the world every where and all the time.

You are so much more than you realize.

Recorded history alone is filled with **achievements** that were once thought to be impossible. Clearly, we are more capable, more creative, and more humane than we are led to believe.

I believe that our collected experience, wisdom, compassion, and creativity can be directed in a way that transforms our environment. We just need some ideas, some motivation, and a different perspective. We can solve any problem, if we **focus more on the solution**. There are plenty of people doing the important work of analyzing what's wrong. That means the rest of us can direct our energy to the cure: flood our world with kindness, appreciation, understanding, curiosity, and programs and incentives that inspire more of the same. It's not rocket science, it's simple math! To *Wow!* our world we need some soul-searching, some healing, and a lot more loving action. We need reminders, role modeling, and way more examples of what's best and what's possible. And that's the fun stuff—thus this list!

By the way, these *101 Ways* include several actions that relate to **children** because that's where we all start. It serves us well to remember how precious we were, whether we felt it or not. And then there are children all around us to whom we have a greater-good responsibility. So use the child-centric items as a guide on how to respond to the children in your life, whether the interaction is fleeting or long term, or whether that child stands in front of you or lives within you.

I have a mug on my desk that's filled with fun pens. You know the ones—topped with flowers, a light-up smiley face, a pinwheel, an alien-looking head with lots of orange tentacles—they make me smile. In fact, the mug is imprinted with a smiling sun and the phrase *Best Day Ever!*—not the result of an achievement, mind you, but as a reminder of the potential in this day.

This book is all about **your potential**, regardless and including the challenges you've faced. I know it sounds like a lot, but I absolutely believe in the best of you—your magnificence. Are you ready? Let's get to it!

The List

101 Ways to *Wow!* Our World

1. Believe in your potential.
2. Talk and listen to children.
3. Radiate respect.
4. Get involved in your community.
5. Honor the spirit in others.
6. Maintain a daily practice of mindful awareness.
7. Feel you're losing it? …Go for a walk.
8. …Take a bath.
9. …Count to 10, slowly.
10. …Call a friend.
11. …Call a hotline.
12. …Stop. Take 3 slow, deep breaths. Repeat.
13. …Step away.
14. Take a break. Don't break someone's spirit.
15. Speak up for a child.
16. Spare the rod; love the child.
17. Tell someone. Report suspected abuse.
18. Have integrity. Say what you mean, do what you say.
19. Protect all children.
20. Give praise.
21. See a mistake as an opportunity.
22. Be honest with children.
23. Empower victims of domestic violence.
24. Donate the cost of a counseling session.
25. Gift your time, services, money to a vision you support.
26. Discover your sacred space.
27. Join the kindness movement.
28. Make time for the children in your life.
29. Read to a child.
30. Embrace each stage of a child's development.
31. Connect with a mentoring program.
32. Respect the rights of every child.
33. Demonstrate responsibility.
34. Enhance your child caring and awareness skills.
35. Take a communication class.
36. Remember your magnificence.
37. Share your talents.
38. Make it safe to share feelings and ideas.
39. Let fear be a nudge, not an anchor.
40. Resolve old beliefs around power, intimacy, and control.
41. Take an *alternatives to violence* class.
42. Know that asking for help takes courage and demonstrates strength.
43. Heal your wounds. Know you can.
44. Accept the help you deserve.
45. Share your wisdom.

46. Choose your words with care.
47. Engage in healthy play.
48. Do more of what you love.
49. Spend time in nature.
50. Be kind to animals.
51. Support, encourage, and preserve creative expression.
52. Celebrate your efforts.
53. Speak the truth.
54. Ask: What is the loving thing to do?
55. Be an inspiration!
56. Extend courtesy.
57. Create family traditions to cherish.
58. Trust more.
59. Make mealtime a special time to nourish and connect.
60. Teach rather than control.
61. Honor the boundaries of others.
62. Define and defend what is right and true for you.
63. Receive graciously.
64. Say thank you.
65. See children as a gift, yourself as their guide.
66. Be the parent you wish you had.
67. Treat yourself with the respect you deserve.
68. Appreciate the journey.
69. Reconnect with the wonder.
70. Manifest a childhood dream.
71. Learn something new.
72. Revive childlike innocence.
73. Promote peace.
74. Contact your legislators.
75. Get involved in the legal system.
76. Participate in the political process.
77. Increase joy. Decrease violence.
78. Rethink, redefine, recycle.
79. Model the behavior you want to see.
80. Explore the true meaning of love.
81. Know that *Love* never hurts.
82. Be curious.
83. Turn conflict into a shared accomplishment.
84. Release the (k)nots.
85. Care more.
86. Forgive yourself.
87. Cultivate a positive outlook.
88. Smile more.
89. Begin each day knowing you make a difference.
90. Get moving!
91. Focus on peace. Focus on compassion.
92. Gather for a common cause.
93. Promote equality, inclusion, and cooperation.
94. Renew your spirit.
95. Delight in the abundance.
96. Expect miracles.
97. Make wishes.
98. Be part of the solution.
99. Share this list.
100. Create your own list.
101. Love more.

101 Ways

1

Believe in your potential.

An acorn has nearly all it needs to grow into a giant oak. It won't change into a willow tree, a turtle, or a rose. It will remain true to its destiny—that of an oak. We, too, have a natural born capacity for coming into being, an ability to grow into the person we envision. Our soul's wish, our true nature, our deepest desire come with the ability to make it happen. It might require special training and financial assistance, but when we recognize and accept what makes us feel vibrantly alive, doors will open that we never thought possible. It's not about having something to prove. It's about being authentic and recognizing our value and the gifts we have to share. That is our potential. Believe in your brightest future possible and let that light guide you forward.

For more context, see 36. Magnificence.[1]

---

[1] These notes refer to other Ways in this book that may provide more context or inspiration. For example, "36. Magnificence" is a shortened reference to 36. Remember your magnificence.

2

Talk and listen to children.

Children—in your care or in public spaces—deserve to be heard. Our response provides an example of respect and caring that helps them grow into responsible adults. Show that their ideas, concerns, and feelings matter by talking with them. It doesn't have to be a formal discussion. Cooking, cleaning the garage, playing a game, or walking the dog can create a shared space for easy conversation. More often than not, when they come to you with a question—or for any reason—stop what you're doing, turn and face them, and look directly into their eyes. Give them your full attention. Mute or turn off the TV. Silence your cell phone. To the child this says: I see you, I'm listening, I want to hear what you have to say, and you are important to me. By the way, it's the same for adults.

3

Radiate respect.

Treat others as if you value or admire their opinions, actions, ideas, feelings, wishes, and presence. It's what we expect in return, as if we too are worthy of consideration, and our points of view—even if different—have merit.

Respect is not about fear or control; it's all about acknowledging one's natural, unconditional worth and right to be. Respect is not forced; it's gifted.

Radiate respect in everything you do and you'll likely encounter more respectful interaction everywhere you go.

4

Get involved in your community.

Participate in and support local events. Attend a meeting, join a committee or enrichment activity and contribute to the safety, beauty, unity, and friendliness of your community. Check your city's library or chamber of commerce for resources and contacts. Search the Internet with terms like *community building* or *neighborhood enrichment ideas*. Share your enthusiasm! (For more ideas, see 92. Gather.) Here are three sites to get you started![2]

National Crime Prevention Council: neighborhood programs and resources.   ncpc.org[3]

Neighborhood Day: tips on gathering and being more neighborly.   neighborhoodday.org

Do Something: young people working for positive change in their communities.   dosomething.org

---

[2] More on these and others in the Resources section.
[3] All website listings appear in short form (minus the preceding https://www).

Library

While libraries are the great keepers of books, library staff are often trained in information studies. They thrive on knowing and locating information to assist their patrons in exploring topics and solving search issues. They often hold classes, workshops, and other special events and may be looking for topics of interest to share with the community. Your question may inspire an event!

At Work

Talk to the events coordinator, human resources person, or your boss. They may be looking for new and creative ways to bring more people skills to the workplace or engage in community action.

5

Honor the spirit in others.

Namaste (nah-muh-stay) is a Sanskrit (ancient language) word used as a salutation of respect and reverence. There are variations on the translation but the essence is the same: the spirit within me bows to the spirit within you, suggesting an acceptance without judgment of the soul in one by the soul in another. It embodies the idea that we are all spiritual beings sharing in this earthly adventure. **The gesture**: bring your hands together in front of your heart (or at the brow level, then to your heart), palms pressing softly into each other, fingers touching and pointing upward. Bow your head and say *Namaste* or let the gesture imply it.[4]

Consider being more mindful in your interactions by looking beyond others' beliefs, actions, accomplishments, challenges, and words to that part of them that is whole, loving, and complete—their spiritual essence. When you look in the mirror, honor that same spirit in you. *Namaste*.

---

[4] Jenae, *Your Light, Your Life!*

6

Maintain a daily practice of mindful awareness.

It's easy to get caught up in the problems and drama around us, so it's important to learn methods to disconnect from all the noise and reconnect to the love within. **Meditation** is an intentional practice to calm the mind, open the heart, expand awareness, and more. Typically, the focus is turned inward for a few minutes or much longer. **Mindfulness** is the opposite of multi-tasking and involves full awareness of your thoughts, feelings, and behavior in the present moment. With some dedication, both practices become easier to achieve. Explore one that works best for you. The better you feel, the more you reflect that state into your interactions and your environment. And the more graciously present you are, the less likely for tension to build.

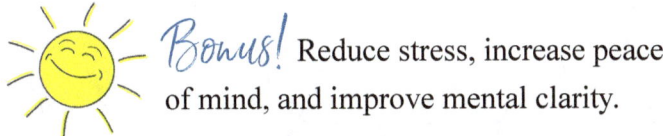 *Bonus!* Reduce stress, increase peace of mind, and improve mental clarity.

Mindful Moment

Remember the last time you were so caught up in an activity that you lost track of time? Maybe you were practicing some dance moves, painting a picture, or sitting by the lake. That feeling of "being one with" is the sweet spot you're looking for, where all your attention is drawn to the wonder of the present moment.

Thailand

7

Feel you're losing it? ...Go for a walk.

Your response to a situation is ultimately under your control, and you may have more options than you think. If those in your care are safe, a walk can clear your head, release some energy, and open a space for answers you may be seeking. If you can't leave your home or workplace, release some energy by cleaning something or just stepping outside for some fresh air and some deep breathing. Walk around the block, walk around the building. You can take a time-out, too, and in the process you demonstrate thoughtful action.

8

...Take a bath.

Let a warm bath or shower relax your body, deepen your breathing, slow your heart rate, and calm you down. Visualize the tension washing away. Replace it with the delight and comfort of memories you cherish. Soak in the positive emotions that you now choose to feel. Allow yourself to decompress so your interaction with another is considerate, appropriate, and wise.

The cure to feeling a loss of control is to do something that brings <u>you</u> back to your center.

9

…Count to 10, slowly.

Place your hand over your heart and count down from 10 to 1, slowly and mindfully. Focus on each number as you remember something you are grateful for outside of the current situation. Pause to picture what you treasure about each one. Let that goodness spread throughout your being and help you relax. Or, consider the qualities you want to engage, such as patience, kindness, calm, clarity, ease. Count them off—perhaps remembering a time when you embodied that quality—knowing by the time you get to 1, you will be more at ease and able to respond in the best way to this situation. Repeat as needed.

10

…Call a friend.

Make sure this is someone you feel is truly supportive of you. Specifically, their actions, behavior, and words should demonstrate a true interest in your well-being. Don't expect someone who has typically not been there for you to suddenly listen, show concern, and offer some encouragement or advice. Maybe you just want to vent. Ask a friend if they can be that person you call when you need to gain some composure. You may not be ready to talk about the issue, but reach out. Sometimes all we need is the soothing presence of someone who cares to help us feel more grounded and in control.

11

...Call a hotline.

Call lines, such as hotlines, helplines, and warmlines were formed to help people get assistance when it's needed most. Their services differ. Some have counselors by phone, text, or email. Many are available 24/7. All have people who want to help, and many of those, just like you, have needed someone to talk to and are now able to help others. Comfort and information can be a phone call away. Whether it's for you or someone you care about, make the call!

Identify a hot–, help–, warm–, or information line (for examples, see Resources: CALL and FIND) that fits your situation or concern. Even if you're not ready to call or just want to learn more, there's peace of mind in knowing you have options. Flag the relevant page in this book or add the phone number/website to your personal list of Important Numbers (see back pages for a sample).

Before Make a list of contacts that are important to your situation. Keep a copy where you can find it in a hurry, such as in your wallet, cell phone, or taped inside a kitchen cabinet. Be sure to identify someone who can step in if you need to step away. In an emergency, you'll be glad you did. (For more list ideas, see 13. Step away, 94. Renew.)

During Remember that you have options. Take some deep breaths then check your list of contacts. If you call and get a recording, don't give up! Leave a message or disconnect, wait a few seconds and call again; or try another contact. It's okay to reach out to others, even strangers, in an emergency. After all, your best friend was once a stranger to you.

After Review the crisis: how it unfolded, how it was handled, and what you could do differently if it happens again. Revise your lists accordingly. Consider contacting a social service agency for more ideas. It's what they do!

12

...Stop. Take 3 slow, deep breaths. Repeat.

No doubt your heart is racing, and you're taking in shorter breaths—typical responses to high stress. Take in a huge deep breath—into your belly—then let it out slowly. Your first attempt may feel awkward and likely won't have much noticeable effect, so take in a second deep breath. Hold it for a couple beats then exhale slower than the inhale. Make the third one deeper and more mindful, releasing any unease. Repeat this process until you feel calmer. Close your eyes, turn away, leave the room. Do what you can to help this technique work, because it will work!

Why? When you are relaxed and content and take in a deep breath, that breath naturally goes into your belly. Mindful belly breathing (vs. chest) stimulates the vagus nerve[5] signaling a state of rest and safety. You can activate this relaxation response in times of stress by consciously breathing deep into your belly until you feel more at ease. It's one of our superpowers!

---
[5] Solan, "Ease anxiety and stress."

13

...Step away.

Sometimes, instead of thinking a situation through, we over-react or act too quickly out of anger, fear, or frustration. If you are prone to respond in a physically harmful way, then your immediate action should be to move away from your child, others, or the situation. If those that depend on you are safe, leave the room and collect yourself. Your reaction may be an old pattern that no longer serves you. You can replace that pattern with new responses that lead to more favorable interaction. With practice you develop more life-affirming habits, find yourself less in crisis mode, and more able to handle the challenges that do occur.

When you are not in a crisis, create a list of *positive actions* that you know will help you feel better when tension starts to build. Refer to it at the first signs of stress or negativity. For ideas, see 26. Sacred Space, 49. Nature, 88. Smile, and 94. Renew and Feel Good Journal.

Quick Release

Feeling overwhelmed? Shake your body, like a dog after a swim, and release all that frantic energy. Really get into it! Shake your arms, your legs, your hands, your feet. Keep shaking until you feel the negative release. Let it all go. Now, stand still and visualize a wave of calm confidence filling every part of you, and with it the inspiration to know what is best to do next.

Lithuania

14

Take a break. Don't break someone's spirit.

Next time you start to feel anxious, notice your body's stress signals, which may include increased heart rate, irritability, scattered thinking, negative thoughts, or physical aches. Do you turn to food, alcohol, or drugs when under pressure? Does your mood drop at a specific time of day or around certain people? How about Internet surfing, social media, or watching the news? Identify these triggers early so you can disengage, release an old habit, and bring your mood back into balance. Take a break so you don't take your build-up of stress out on anyone else. This may only take a few minutes, but the heartwarming effect can last all day.

For more ways to engage your inner calm, review 7–13. Losing it, 49. Nature, 84. Knots, and 94. Renew.

15

Speak up for a child.

Children often lack the experience, understanding, or command of the language to express themselves when needed. And because they are children, sometimes adults don't listen. But as adults, it is our responsibility to speak on behalf of a child's well-being. From reporting harmful behavior (see 17. Tell someone), raising funds for a youth center, helping a lost child, to speaking up for them in a room crowded with adults—find your voice! There are many opportunities on local or international levels in such areas as education, law, safety, community, literacy, and health.

Give children a reason to believe that there are many caring adults in the world.

For ideas, see Resources: Volunteer.

16

Spare the rod; love the child.

Physical discipline, including the use of an object (belt, wooden spoon, stick), is more about punishment through pain than a desire to promote positive and acceptable behavior and interaction. Fueled by anger and frustration, slapping, hitting, or spanking promotes fear, distrust, and distance between adult and child, teaching violence as a tool to resolve conflict. Consequences may be necessary, but the goal is to foster understanding and encourage better choices. Striking a child is a violation of their space, their spirit, their trust, their being. Just as no one should ever strike you, never hit a child. Peace begins with you. Seek out loving solutions. They do exist. Your child will love you for it.

For more **context and insight**, see 2. Talk and listen, 14. Take a break, 30. Embrace each stage, 40. Resolve old beliefs, and 81. *Love* never hurts.

For **positive parenting tips**, see Resources: Parents & Caregivers, or use *positive parenting* in your Internet search.

Do This, Not That

Discipline means to teach. To achieve loving results, we teach through loving action.

- Model and acknowledge positive and respectful behavior.
- Set and enforce clear rules and limits.
- Plan ahead. Provide opportunities for success.

The United Nations Committee on the Rights of the Child defines corporal or physical punishment "as any punishment in which physical force is used and intended to cause some degree of pain or discomfort, however light."[6]

- Corporal punishment is the most common form of violence against children worldwide.
- 68 UN countries have banned all corporal punishment of children, including in the home.[7]
- In the United States (US), corporal punishment is banned in some settings but NOT in the home.[8]

---

[6] United Nations, UN Committee, General Comment.
[7] End Corporal Punishment, "Reforming National Laws…" Settings include: home, alternative care, daycare, schools, penal institutions, sentencing.
[8] Visit EndCorporalPunishment.org for more on this important topic.

17

Tell someone.
Report suspected abuse.

Some people hesitate to report.

Why? They may be afraid of over-reacting, hope someone else will do it, think it won't do any good, or just don't want to get involved. But if nothing is done, then someone is not safe. Meanwhile, the abusive dynamic is growing stronger in the family, the abuser is getting away with it and getting more out of control, and the victim is getting more frightened, more threatened, and may become self-destructive or hurtful to others. The entire family feels the effects and may respond in different ways including denial, withdrawal, or repeating the harmful behavior they see. Make the call!

See Resources: CALL, and for more context see Reach Out: About Reporting.

Police Welfare Check

Concerned about the well-being of a neighbor, child, friend or relative? Consider calling their local police (not 911) and request a *welfare* or *wellness check* to have an officer stop by and check on their safety. To learn more, search the Internet for *police welfare check*. To find local police, search USA.gov.

Signal for Help

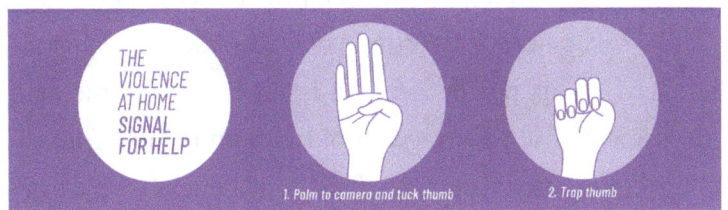

A victim's silent call for help or support may involve gestures not intended to be noticed by everyone. The above trapped thumb *Signal for Help* was created for on-line use but is also used offline and in public spaces. To learn more, visit CanadianWomen.org. To see a video of *the Signal* in action, use the direct link below or search a video channel or the Internet for *Signal for Help*.
https://www.youtube.com/watch?v=AFLZEQFIm7k

18

Have integrity. Say what you mean, do what you say.

Keep your promises. Avoid saying you'll do something if you know you're not likely to deliver.

Why? Over time, your lack of action teaches that you are not trustworthy; you do not do or mean what you say. If this has become an issue for you, some self-assessment could identify an old pattern or belief that is contributing to your choices. Awareness welcomes change.

How? Next time, pause before you act. Decide what you are willing and able to do in this situation. Speak the truth, respond from the heart. Be the dependable person you know yourself to be.

19

Protect all children.

Step in if you see a child being bullied, whether by peers or adults. Demonstrate that this conduct is never okay. Act immediately and be respectful, even if all you can do is provide a distraction to break the mood. If you see a child doing something unsafe (i.e., too close to the edge, playing with matches) and the parent is absent or doesn't notice, say something (without criticism or blame), do something. Step up and move the child to safety or remove the dangerous item. Sometimes, we are not sure what to do and the moment passes. Prepare yourself! Identify your concern—bullying, abuse in public, dangerous activity—and contact a related organization for ideas or referrals. Seek out a range of possibilities so the next time that situation presents itself, you'll have more options. Want some ideas? Visit StopBullying.gov or use *bystander intervention* as your Internet search term.

Children are new to the planet.
We do not own them. We are
their guardians and their guides.
We get to cherish them.

Belarus

20

Give praise.

Give genuine praise when praise is due, but make it appropriate. A child's view of clean is probably different from yours. Be reasonable. Consider their age, experience, and level of development. Provide a specific instruction (i.e. move all toys to the toy box; all clothes off the floor and into the laundry basket) that clarifies the result you want to achieve or lesson you are trying to teach.

We all want to feel appreciated for who we are and what we do. So be sure to praise the positive behavior you see, regardless of where you see it. This inspires more of the same.

For more inspiration, refer to 60. Teach, 64. Thank, 65. Gift, 66. Parent.

21

See a mistake as an opportunity.

We can become unyielding in our plans and expectations leaving little room for spontaneity. But if we view a decision that ultimately had an unwanted effect as a mark against our character, we miss the opportunity to learn something new. Anger over a wrong turn, a traffic jam, or at other drivers doesn't change the traffic, it just changes the atmosphere around you. And, although that wrong turn may have resulted in "lost" time, it may have taken you out of harm's way or enabled you to enjoy a route you would not have taken. Don't let a mistake or an unexpected event ruin your whole day and that of those around you. Allow the change to be a blessing in disguise, whether or not you ever see it.

22

Be honest with children.

Children can handle the truth if delivered with compassion[9] and age appropriateness. There may be times when the truth has to wait but, as a rule, honesty is the best policy. Even a difficult question (have you ever smoked pot or lied to your parents) requires an honest response not a lecture or a defensive attitude. Remember, it's not about you! And what an opportunity to open a dialog. You don't have to cover the entire subject in one sitting, but your willingness to talk with them opens a door to future questions and discussions on topics they may struggle with and need your wise counsel. You may find that their interests or concerns are similar to those you had at their age. In these moments you teach what you give. An honest answer from you—and they will know when you are telling the truth—is far more likely to elicit an honest answer and conversation with them.

---

[9] Compassion: a nonjudgmental awareness and understanding of the feelings and suffering of others and wanting to do something about it; active caring.

23

Empower victims of domestic violence.

On a **personal** level: remind survivors[10] of their strength, persistence, and creativity, because that's some of what it takes to endure a toxic relationship. Listen, actively care, and ask what you can do to help. If needed, assist them in creating a safety plan (See 62. Define and Defend, and Safety Planning). In **general**: consider donating time, services, or money to safe places for victims to recover. Shelters provide space for women and children who choose to leave a dangerous living situation, a choice often made suddenly and with little planning. Visit DomesticShelters.org to locate a program or shelter and access other empowering resources for victims to make a fresh and healthy start. Empower survivors, empower the world! For more context, see 93. Promote Equality.

---

[10] Offenders may also be victims of domestic violence and need assistance with old beliefs and new healthy patterns. See #40–45, and Reach Out for more on that.

24

Donate the cost
of a counseling session.

Counseling can be an important process in healing from any trauma, but for some, the cost is an obstacle they cannot get beyond. Contact a local therapy program and see how a specific donation might work. You might choose a focus—abuse, alcohol, drugs, violence, depression—that has affected you in some way.

Imagine a client appearing for an appointment to find that the fee has already been paid; in fact, the entire month has been covered! Consider remaining anonymous, because it's not about the thanks—that will be there. It's all about the smile, the sigh of relief, or the thoughtful gaze as they wonder who could have given such a kindhearted gift.

25

Give your time, services, money to a vision you support.

Charitable organizations are formed to address a public concern. Their survival depends on funding from a variety of sources, public or private. Choose one or several that have meaning for you. Call and ask what services they need and offer what fits your schedule from yard work and painting to office skills or financial contributions. Consider joining their board or be on a committee. From disaster relief to chambers of commerce, museums, animal shelters, and community arts, there are many organizations that could use your skills, your time, and your contribution.

You're in good company: Approximately 63 million Americans (25% of adults) volunteer their time, talents, and energy to make a positive difference.[11] WOW!

---

[11] Nonprofits Source, "Volunteering Statistics."

26

Discover your sacred space.

In your favorite chair or corner of a room, on a rope swing or garden bench, on the grass under a tree, or on the front porch at night. Maybe it's the way that space lights up with the morning sun streaming through the window. Maybe it's not a visual thing; it just *feels* special.

Freshen it up, toss some pillows into it, rearrange the elements of it, and honor this place. It doesn't have to be a decorator's haven, it doesn't have to have walls, but it does have to feel special to you. It might be at the park, your favorite view spot, or on your morning walk, but identify a place (or two) where you can tune in to the loving energy in your world. Your sacred space may be holding ideas just waiting for you to capture.

27

Join the kindness movement.

A thoughtful act benefits the receiver and all who witness it, but studies also show that deliberately engaging in acts of kindness promotes mental, emotional, and physical health. Start your day, conversation, trip to the store, and any interaction with a conscious awareness of being more kind. Say hello to simply acknowledge the presence of others on a walk, in the store, waiting in line. Need more ideas? Go to RandomActsofKindness.org or use *acts of kindness* as your Internet search term. Start a list of do-able actions that resonate with you. Plan ahead and calendar a Kindness Day! Include children in your kindness campaign. They may know a person or family that could use a boost. Kindness is normal, rewarding, and uplifting. Kindness is contagious.

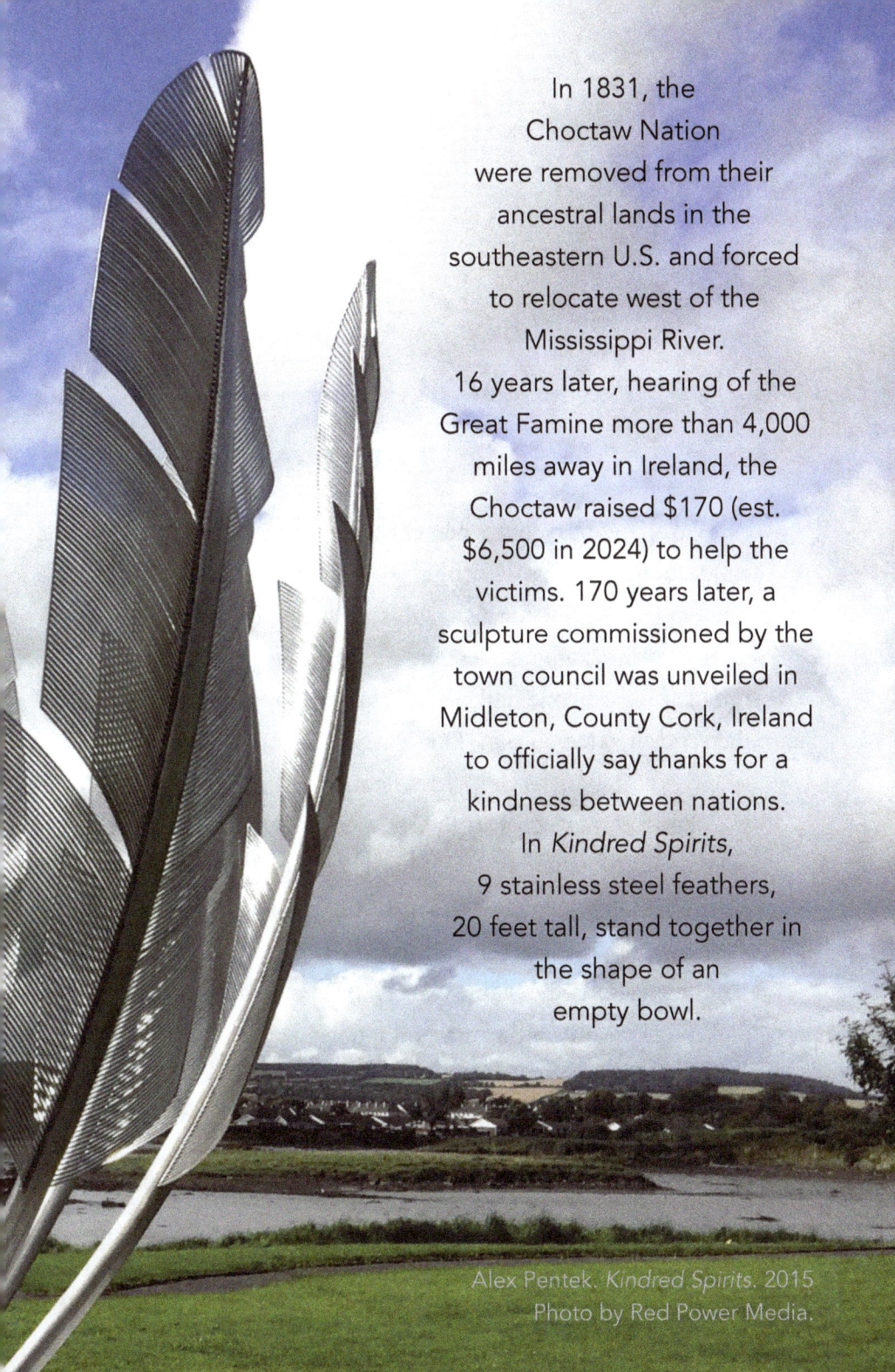

In 1831, the Choctaw Nation were removed from their ancestral lands in the southeastern U.S. and forced to relocate west of the Mississippi River. 16 years later, hearing of the Great Famine more than 4,000 miles away in Ireland, the Choctaw raised $170 (est. $6,500 in 2024) to help the victims. 170 years later, a sculpture commissioned by the town council was unveiled in Midleton, County Cork, Ireland to officially say thanks for a kindness between nations. In *Kindred Spirits*, 9 stainless steel feathers, 20 feet tall, stand together in the shape of an empty bowl.

Alex Pentek. *Kindred Spirits*. 2015
Photo by Red Power Media.

28

Make time for the children in your life.

We all get busy, but when children approach you with a question or activity, recognize that they have singled you out as someone to trust. If it is truly inconvenient, ask them to wait (examples: ten minutes to finish a report, five minutes for a phone call, or later in the day after work) then stick to what you say. Don't offer it if you don't mean it. (See 18. Integrity.) Help them learn to respect your time by showing respect for theirs. And make time now because this time will pass. Play with your children. Show a genuine interest in their life and, if appropriate, include them in your projects. Schedule time together: homework, family meals, game nights, outdoors. Be available. Be present. Remember how important it was to you as a child.

29

Read to a child.

Set aside time, regularly, to read to your young child. Allow no distractions. In the process you encourage them to read, listen, and think on their own. Plus, it offers a time for you to feel close, to bond, and to talk as questions arise, even on unrelated topics. It also reinforces the importance of reading as a life-long tool to gain knowledge, understanding, and excite the imagination.

And, let a child read to you. Demonstrate trust and an interest in their ability and process. Allow them to share with you all those positive vibes they get when you read to them. Awesome!

Visit your local library. You can borrow, read, and return for more. And many libraries have reading programs looking for more readers just like you.

30

Embrace each stage of a child's development.

Childhood is a time of immense imagination, exploration, and discovery—qualities that serve us well into adulthood, but only if we cultivate and trust them. Sometimes, in wanting what's best for a child, we push him to excel, involve her in too many activities, and expect them to be little adults. Our role is to be aware and respond according to their level of understanding. We may think a child is very mature for his age, but he is still a child exploring his world and often mirroring what he sees. And when, as a teen, she distances herself from us, it may not be about us at all, but her need for autonomy. Our goal is to enable them to live independent, authentic, and fulfilling lives. So let kids be kids, with all the curiosity and creativity they can muster. Don't rush them through this time. They are learning more than you know, while you provide the balance between structure and freedom that they need.

31

Connect with a mentoring program.

Young people need guidance. Many come from homes with absent or troubled parents or guardians who have not been exposed to healthy life patterns. Your advice and life lessons could be exactly what's needed for a person navigating the world of relationships, school, or transition to college and work. More than anything, you can be the one who listens and cares.

Check the Resources: Volunteer and Youth sections to sign up, contribute to, or find more opportunities in your area. Here are three to get you started.

Boys and Girls Clubs of America — bgca.org

Mentor — mentoring.org

Idealist — idealist.org

32

Respect the rights of every child.

Children everywhere have the same rights as adults to health, happiness, safety, and freedom of expression. They, like us, want to feel loved, accepted, and safe. Next time you are in the vicinity of any child, in public or private, be mindful of their presence and their potential. Consider, too, that one day their ideas and perspectives may burst into existence in the best of ways if we guide them with our caring, appreciation, and sensitivity. Children are not *our* future. They deserve our respect simply because they are here.

Child Rights

The United Nations Convention on the Rights of the Child is the most widely ratified human rights treaty in history. It is well worth the read and our active support! Visit UNICEF.org for reader-friendly versions. See Further Reading: UN Documents for more about this historic commitment to the world's children.

33

Demonstrate responsibility.

We have all looked to others to show us how to act in unfamiliar territory. Children, by nature, turn to adults for guidance, approval, and protection. Adults teach responsible action by being trustworthy, sensible, reliable, and protective.

How? Demonstrate the ability to respond with fairness, compassion, and wisdom. Be mindful of others' culture, traditions, opinion, gender, age, skill level, and beliefs. Admit when you're wrong. Say you're sorry when you know your words or actions have been hurtful. Seek assistance when you need it. You don't have to know all the answers, but you can take action to find them, and that teaches resourcefulness.

Remember, you are not responsible for everything and everyone. Just as your behavior, decisions, and lessons are your own, let others claim responsibility for what is theirs.

34

Enhance your child caring and awareness skills.

Children do not arrive with a one-size-fits-all instruction manual—there are far too many variables, but there are fundamental and valuable guidelines. Often you need to trust your instincts—that inner knowing—on what is best for the children you encounter or those in your care. Take a child care/development/parenting class or read a book on the same. Engage with organizations that research and post tips and tools for this purpose, like: Parent/Teacher organizations, social services, and healing centers. Remember to resolve any of your childhood pain points so you don't pass them on.

See 65. Gift, 66. Parent, and Resources: Parents & Caregivers for more ideas.

35

Take a communication class.

Communication takes many forms and, with so many beings on the planet, it may be the most important skill we learn. Whether we realize it or not, we continually monitor for emotional cues by watching, listening, and sensing what others feel. And we don't all speak the same emotional language. Some are better at it than others, so it can only benefit us to learn more.

Explore new methods to express yourself because the more skilled you become, the more confidence you will have in relating to others. Need some motivation? Try writing, painting, dancing, singing, acting, public speaking, or languages. Check your community and college calendars for events. If you ever have difficulty conveying an idea or emotion, imagine what it might be like for others, especially a child, to find the right words.

Handwriting is a form of communication that is unique to the individual, and its use exercises the brain! So grab some paper and your favorite pens or pencils and write out your thoughts and ideas. No editing! By writing freely about a topic or concern, you may discover a solution or simply feel better getting it out of your head. You can also fill a page with positive statements about you, your situation, your goals and abilities—and use it to rewire your brain for more fulfilling results. *Write On!*

36

Remember your magnificence.

It's true! We are born with this awareness, this unlimited joy of being, this bursting, buzzing potential of aliveness. But sometimes we forget. Too many challenges and disappointments can do that and may have created a belief that any pain, harm, or injustice is a burden we have to carry for the rest of our lives. But what if that history provided the training, foundation, and best perspective for our love (source) and light (expression) to manifest? Your magnificence is not about ego. It is simply who and what you are beyond all the random stuff of this life. That love, that worthiness, untouched by measure or comparison, is your essence. Your magnificence is that light of pure loving energy that, if you let it, radiates freely from you. Remember, too, that this source is in every one, every thing, every where, and all the time.[12]

---

[12] Jenae, *Your Light, Your Life!*

37

Share your talents.

Pass along your gifts—those talents you were born with or acquired along the way. You don't have to be a best-selling author to share your writing and captivate your readers. You don't have to be on the music industry's top 10 list to delight an audience with your voice or your melodies. Share what you love to do!

How? Become a tutor and share the knowledge that came easy for you. Consider a skills swap for a win-win talent trade. Check your local community, senior, or youth centers for programs and opportunities. Lots of groups are looking for volunteers and speakers to share their skills. Connect! Have an idea but can't find a group? Start one! There is an appreciative audience waiting. See Resources: Volunteer for more ideas.

38

Make it safe to share feelings and ideas.

It starts with a connection, like eye contact and words that indicate genuine concern. Look at the person you are talking to with interest. Turn toward them. Let them see that you care about what they have to say. Ask questions, then—and this is important—wait for the answer and respond accordingly. Know that when a problem is shared, you don't have to fix it. Sometimes we just need to listen, show that we care, and let others find their own way.

In a family, at work, or in any relationship, set aside a regular (daily, weekly, monthly) time slot to talk about news, ideas, issues, or to celebrate each other. Remember to establish device-free zones (see 56. Courtesy and E-Etiquette) and fully engage with the people around you. It's the emotional connections we long for and the ones we'll treasure. In the process, you teach the same respect you show. Wow!

39

Let fear be a nudge, not an anchor.

Fear is a tremendous act of love. It serves to protect our core—that loving essence—from immediate danger. It also provides a nudge, a reminder of the *possibility* of emotional or physical harm.

As a nudge, fear offers the opportunity to make a thoughtful choice. It says, "Excuse me. May I interrupt your flow for just a minute and remind you of the last time you did that?" It's not saying don't do it. It's just asking you to pause and consider that in a similar situation you had a discomforting result. You don't want to anchor that fear by giving it too much attention, because then it works overtime preventing you from <u>any</u> possible risk. Instead, acknowledge its presence, appreciate the intention, release the fear, and embrace the potential in your current situation. Move forward, not back. You got this!

40

Resolve old beliefs around power, intimacy, and control.

Issues with power (our sense of ability, value, confidence), intimacy (emotional closeness, connection, and communication), and control (over ourselves and our environment) are often a reflection of repeated harmful behavior that we lived with in some way. Unresolved, we might treat ourselves or others similarly in a subconscious attempt to heal what should never have happened. Sexual, physical, and emotional abuse of any person is not about "teaching" or "discipline." It's about taking advantage and should not be tolerated. Abusive behavior is a result of fear—of lack, of feeling unworthy, of a loss of a sense of self. That fear may have created patterns that can be identified and resolved, while engaging more loving and empowering interaction—something every relationship needs. See Reach Out, and browse the Resources section for organizations related to this topic.

41

Take an *alternatives to violence* class.

The title may be different but the point is to learn how to resolve issues without inflicting harm. The need is clear. Too many people have been exposed to violent behavior in the family, in public, or through media outlets. Some have never witnessed calm, responsive, and inclusive interaction in working through disagreements; so their immediate reaction is to repeat the patterns they know, and those actions may be aggressive, harmful, and dangerous. There are more productive ways and, with practice, they will replace some old conditioning that is enabling the cycle of violence that has become familiar. Life is all about relationships! To have the best, we make healthier choices and apply new skills. Search for *alternatives to violence, conflict resolution, positive relations* or contact a hotline for suggestions and programs near you. See 40. Resolve, and Resources: Healthy Mind, Body, Spirit for more.

42

Know that asking for help takes courage and demonstrates strength.

It may seem like giving up control, but the truth is it takes courage to explore new worlds and it takes strength to face the monsters that appear on the journey. True also that you have the courage and strength you need to face any challenge. Those two qualities and more have gotten you this far and, with a new perspective, can now be applied to more rewarding endeavors. Contact a hotline, counseling center, or an issue related group and ask about their process, expectations, and the philosophy and goal of the counselor, instructor, or group leader. (See Reach Out.) This *is* taking control of your life and the direction in which you are headed. Why not aim for the best result? It's more than possible. The first step is under your feet!

43

Heal your wounds.
Know you can.

If you fall and scrape your knee, your body responds to the damage by sending in various aids to promote recovery. Emotional wounds also need to be recognized so they can heal, and that attention comes from you. You have to acknowledge that they exist, identify the source, how it's affected you, and your role (if any) in it. Your part may simply have been that you were there, not that it was your fault. At some point, when you're ready to stop being hurt by it, you can choose to let it go.

After all, that was then. You are now smarter, more mature, stronger, confident, and have more resources available to you to truly heal, transform, and live your best life ever! Make the time. You are worth it! You can do this!

The water lily is rooted in mud, yet it reaches through the darkness of murky waters to bloom into a beautiful flower. The leaves of the water lily rest on the water's surface, perhaps providing additional stability for it to blossom. For that is its destiny—to blossom. Everything else is the adventure of becoming.

44

Accept the help you deserve.

You do not have to do this alone. The only mark against you—by asking for help—is the one you put on yourself.

It takes a long time to build a bridge on your own, yet there are bridge builders who long for the opportunity to share their expertise. If your refrigerator, car, or computer stopped working, you likely wouldn't hesitate to call a repair person, mechanic, or technical adviser. You deserve at least that same level of care and attention.

Make the call! Establish a network of support through caring people and organizations. (For ideas and a nudge, see Reach Out: Counseling.)

The sooner you get through, the more time you will have to build a life to cherish.

45

Share your wisdom.

The idea of helping others resolve issues that you, too, have endured is a noble one. First, do your healing work.

Knowledge & Experience + Understanding
= Wisdom

You can write or talk about your story. You can become a counselor, lawyer, or doctor on related concerns. You can be a mentor, an advocate, or a group facilitator. You can simply and importantly be a friend with a sympathetic ear, but first, resolve any negative patterns and limiting beliefs from the past; don't carry them forward. Because the recovery work you do—reclaiming your authentic self—will give you the foundation, tools, and perspective you need to effectively help someone else.

46

Choose your words with care.

If you use words or actions that belittle, embarrass, or shame, you may be repeating similar behavior that you witnessed or was hurtful to you. And it may have become a habit. You didn't deserve it then, you don't deserve it now, and neither does anyone around you. Explore the source of your pain so you can stop passing it on. Words matter. Choose those that are honest, clear, loving, and supportive. Choose words with positive energy. It's not about denial. It's about being aware of and breaking old destructive thought patterns while taking responsibility for creating the loving life you envision. For more insight, see 67. Treat Yourself, and 87. Cultivate.

47

Engage in healthy play.

Play time is important to a child's development and an adult's mental health, but sometimes a line is crossed between mutual fun and inflicting harm. Endless and repeated criticism, teasing, and tickling isn't pleasant for anyone. It doesn't build strong character and can cause physical, mental, and emotional distress. Healthy play at any age has loads of rewards. It can relieve stress, stimulate the brain, spark creativity, build trust, and often includes grins, giggles, and good times!

Remember, having fun is not the same for everyone but it is important to everyone's well-being.

48

Do more of what you love.

It's easy to get caught up in the cycle of responding to every call for attention. Rather than appear inconsiderate, we set our needs and wishes aside. Too much and we minimize our needs entirely. Eventually, we may feel guilty taking personal time and, instead, fill any quiet (and potentially enlightening) moments with more busyness or mindless input. But if we continue to deny what truly makes us happy, we get out of balance and may soon feel increased frustration, worry, irritability, and illness reminding us that it's time for some self-care, and that involves doing what you love. And, frankly, the world needs more of that because, the more you do what you love, the more you'll love what you do and that energy is contagious and inspiring to others. Start small if you need to, but start somewhere. Uncomfortable? It might just be unfamiliar. You owe it to yourself. This is not about being selfish. It's about being self-aware.

49

Spend time in nature.

Walk in the woods. Kayak a lazy river. Stroll barefoot on the beach. Stretch out on the grass in your backyard. Sit under a tree at the park. Gaze up at the stars from a wide open meadow. Just for a moment, become wildly aware of the life cycle of any creature or plant in your view. They too have everything they need to thrive. They too are living their best life.

We are all a part of this extraordinary place—on this planet, in this universe. And we are all connected, in some way, to everything! Immerse yourself in this knowledge in a casual, mindful, or meditative way as often as you can. Become delightfully aware, again, of that loving source energy that sparkles everywhere while knowing that it also sparkles in you.

 *Bonus!* Lifts your mood, boosts immunity, increases vitality, lowers blood pressure. Note: These benefits are similar to 6. Mindful.

50

Be kind to animals.

We live among 2.13 million known species of animals on Earth,[13] each with abilities and rituals we may not fully understand. Animals, like humans, are a marvel of nature and deserve our curiosity, care, and protection. Our awareness and action on their behalf demonstrates a capacity for acceptance and compassion that is often unconditional, even for those life forms that seem so different from us. Consider reflecting on or studying those that interest you or attract your attention in any way. In the process, you may discover more about yourself, your connection to others, as well as the planet, than you ever thought was possible.[14]

---

[13] Ritchie, "How many species."
[14] See Ted Andrews book *Animal-Speak* mentioned in Select Books & Media.

51

Support, encourage, and preserve creative expression.

Studies show that participation in the arts improves academic performance, encourages creativity and innovation, offers healing benefits, strengthens communities, and more.[15] Music, dance, literature, sculpture, drawing, painting, acting are just a few examples of artistic expression. Each and all could easily enhance our lives and inspire others. Support the arts in your community and especially in schools. Use the search phrase *arts in the community* to learn even more about its importance to humanity, and try *arts programs* in *your city* or *county* to get involved at a local level. See Resources: Arts.

---

[15] Cohen, "10 Reasons."

Imagination allows us to see things differently. We may even hear differently. That creative spirit is just waiting for us to listen and then do what we dare to believe is possible.

52

Celebrate your efforts.

We celebrate events like birthdays, anniversaries, holidays, and other milestones, but how often do we take the time to celebrate the little things? Sometimes we get so focused on the big picture that we only see the distance without realizing the seeds we've planted, the kindness we've shown, or the bridges we've crossed. When we acknowledge even the little miracles, we clear a path and honor the chance to experience many more. So throw a little party, do a happy dance, or simply mark the moment with mindful, innerwhelming, heartwarming appreciation. A cupcake is also a nice touch. =)[16]

---

[16] Jenae, *Your Light, Your Life!*

53

Speak the truth.

It's not always easy, but it is a worthy goal. What if your words may hurt? You're not responsible for the feelings of others, but you are responsible to consider your intention before you speak. Choose words to match that spirit. Speaking the truth allows the receiver a chance to reconsider, gain a new perspective, or simply understand an opinion. But it works both ways. The truth can open a path to healing, even through discomfort. And we may all remember a time when a truth was told and we wished we had known or done so sooner. Honesty and sincerity are foundational aspects to a strong relationship. Their roles in your history are worthy of reflection.

54

Ask: What is the loving thing to do?

Sometimes we get caught up in fear and start questioning our abilities and intentions. We don't want to do the wrong thing and we worry what others might think, especially if it's in response to someone else's words or behavior. Doubt creeps in resulting in indecision and inaction. At times like these: stop, shake off the anxiety, and take a few deep breaths until you feel more settled. Then ask yourself, *what is the loving thing to do in this situation?* The answer may not come right away. It may also appear as an image or an instinct to do something unrelated, but pay attention because the answer will come. How will you know if it's the loving thing to do? It will feel good in a heartfelt way.

55

Be an inspiration!

To inspire in the best possible way, you simply need to be authentic. Do you believe in an idea, project, or process that could contribute to the greater good?

Share your thoughts!

Have you confronted a fear, broken a habit, followed a dream, achieved the impossible, found a better way?

Share your journey!

Your story may be the perfect story to renew trust, revive hope, or summon the courage to act. Be the love and let that light radiate everywhere. Be an inspiration!

56

Extend courtesy.

Simple friendly gestures are a gift to the recipient and a model of kindness to the observer. Dropped packages? Help pick them up. Someone seem lost or confused? Ask if they need directions. Let a shopper go ahead of you in line at the market. Wave to let others through in traffic or to say thanks when they do the same for you. Be on time for an appointment, call if you will be late, offer to reschedule. Be polite in speech and action. Don't interrupt. Excuse yourself for leaving early, or for crossing in front of someone. Avoid foul language. Say please. Return what you borrow. Care for the property of others. Write and send a note of thanks, cheer, congratulations, or heartfelt wishes.

Often our actions *do* speak louder than words.

E-Etiquette

Be present and courteous in the company of others. Show that their presence matters more by giving them your undivided attention. Put away your gaming devices, tablets, laptops, etc. Turn off the TV. Regarding cell phones:

- Avoid personal calls when you're in spaces like the market or standing in line. Wait till you get outside.

- Keep your phone out of sight when you're with family, in a meeting, or out with a friend.

- Silence your phone in the company of others.

- If you're expecting a call that you must answer, let others know that you may have to step away. Excuse yourself if you must make or take a call.

- Do not put a call on speaker unless you plan to include others in the call. Be sure to let the caller know the conversation can be overheard.

Declare an e-free day and enjoy the opportunity to fully interact in-person with others.

57

Create family traditions to cherish.

Identify activities that your family enjoys doing together and schedule them regularly. Celebrations, after-dinner walks, game night, spring cleaning, holiday preparation, and a community volunteer day are some of the many possibilities for creating a fun or heartfelt tradition. Expect and accept full participation and input. Be open to change. Often it's the simple things we do together that we remember most.

Resistance? Talk through it and especially why it's important to you. Remember that, as the adult, you set the example. Mark your calendar. Open a channel to create memories your family will cherish.

58

Trust more.

Sometimes, we have to trust in the process knowing that, somehow, we're right where we need to be. A series of disappointments can certainly affect our trust reserve, but let it be temporary. Shake off the hurt, learn from the experience, grow in compassion, and move on.

Believe in our humanity, in our ability to improve, to solve problems, to make amends, to live in harmony. Choose to live in the abundant present, acknowledge the gifts <u>you</u> bring, and know that anything is possible. Trust in yourself, in others, in life's mystery. Trust with all your heart and allow the magic to enter.

Also see 91. Focus, and 95. Abundance.

Magic, as in the absolute delight in the unexpected, or when the elements of a situation combine in a perfectly wonderful way. Like catching this image as the light filters through the trees on to worn steps leading to...

59

Make mealtime a special time to nourish and connect.

Families who regularly eat together with the intention to connect, converse, and enjoy each other notice stronger bonds, improved communication skills, and an increase in self-esteem. You can too! Start by making this time important and more enjoyable. Announce your intention. Be honest, open, and expect everyone to participate in your plan for the health of the family. Create a schedule based on your family dynamic, and insist on everyone's presence. The more time spent, the better. Too late? It's never too late; you just need a different way. Feel stuck? Search the Internet for why family meals are important. Check Resources: Parents & Caregivers for organizations with parenting and relationship ideas.

Table Talk

- Mark your calendar. Make gathering for a meal a regular rather than rare event.

- Be inclusive in meal preparation and cleanup.

- Encourage conversation without judgment.

- Ask others what they think and feel.

- Show that respect is always on the table. Request an apology if someone crosses the line.

- Be present: Turn off the TV, computers, and gaming devices, and ban cell phones because this time is family time!

60

Teach rather than control.

Teaching involves communicating information so that others can learn and benefit. Control, in this context, is about getting our own way to gain or maintain a false sense of power or importance. Sometimes control hides in our desire to be needed. So we do the task for someone or re-do what they have done. This repeated behavior is perceived as a lack of trust in their ability and can result in low self-confidence, dependency, and resentment. Instead, recognize their current level of ability or training, consider their point of view, and have some patience. Remember yourself at that age or in a similar situation. Teach love, respect, and responsibility by your actions, your words, and your presence and become a star in the eyes of your student.

61

Honor the boundaries of others.

Visualize an energy field, an aura, or a perimeter around each body. Think of it as a comfort zone. On a physical level, it defines how close we allow others to get to us. Emotional boundaries work on the inside but also affect physical space. They involve personal rules (often unspoken) of safety, courtesy, emotional security, and how we want to be treated. Simply put, honor the boundaries of others by respecting their needs, wishes, and the space they inhabit. Be alert to their signals of discomfort and respond accordingly. The concept of boundaries is well worth exploring. Being more aware and showing more respect will lead to healthier and more fulfilling choices and experiences.

62

Define and defend what is right and true for you.

How about the space you inhabit? Can you say no to an uncomfortable request? Do you know what you want more than what you don't want? Do you communicate your needs clearly? Spend some time with this so you can be clear about what contributes to your sense of safety, well-being, and worthiness. You can choose who, when, how, and if someone touches you. You can walk away from a person who is hurting you physically, emotionally, or psychologically. (See Safety Planning, next page.) Trust your intuition on this one. Not sure? If you initially feel hesitant or distrustful, exercise some caution. It could be an old fear habit or a perception that is spot on. More often than not, your close relationships should be comforting, supportive, considerate, equal, joyful... loving. Learn to be clear about your personal boundaries by being true and respectful to your self. You are worth it!

Safety Planning

Are you in a dangerous or unhealthy relationship and want advice or want to leave? Develop a plan of action. Use *create a safety plan* for your Internet search term. Add *child, domestic violence,* or *work* to be more specific. You are not alone! Here are two places to start:

National Domestic Violence Hotline has an online tool to create a safety plan unique to your situation. Information you enter is not stored on the website. You don't have to complete the plan to use the tool, but each section covers important aspects worthy of review.   thehotline.org

Women's Law has a *Safety Planning* section with tips to stay safe in domestic violence, stalking, social media, and other situations.   womenslaw.org

63

Receive graciously.

Life is a continuous cycle of giving and receiving. Too often suggestions are made that giving is the only way, but giving without ever receiving is unhealthy. And, in order to give, there must be someone on the receiving end accepting what is being offered. Balance is the key. Sometimes we are the giver, sometimes the receiver. Be mindful of both positions for each is a gift to the other. Open your heart and be part of this universal exchange of connection, flow, and abundance.

64

Say thank you.

Notice the kindness of others. Voice your gratitude in person or in writing. It's never too late to be acknowledged, even if the act was a long time ago. Imagine receiving a card, a handwritten note, or a call thanking you—even thanking you again!—for being a treasured friend, for a gift that's made such a difference, or a memorable event that still brings a smile. A sincere thanks is always welcome, and may be received at a time it's needed most—renewing a friendship, lifting a spirit, touching a heart.

It's never too late to say thanks, even to thank someone again. Appreciation is a heart-to-heart connection, and that connection is a smile maker.

65

See children as a gift, yourself as their guide.

Children arrive into a variety of circumstances: some welcoming, some not so much. Yet, like all life on the planet, each is unique and each has value. Children are ready to learn, eager to do well, and want to be appreciated knowing their existence matters—just like adults. They trust us for our knowledge, understanding, encouragement, and protection. Their gift is their presence and all the wonder that brings. Children are new to the planet. We do not own them. We are their guardians and their guides. We get to cherish them.

66

Be the parent you wish you had.

Maybe your parents were great. Do more of what they did. But if you wish your parents had been more available, more playful, loving, open, aware, or in looking back, more insistent on enforcing some rules, be that with the children in your life. It's a simple gauge. When in doubt, reflect back and ask what you would have wanted your parents to do. Trust your instincts. Your parents likely did the best they could with what they knew at the time. Regardless of that result, you can do what you feel is the loving thing to do now. See #54. Ask.

67

Treat yourself with the respect you deserve.

Self-esteem is having confidence in your own worth. This value is not based on what you do, what you have done, or your good intentions. You have value simply because you are here. You can always change what you do. You can also change habits and beliefs, but underneath it all is that essence that is you.

Your life matters. You matter, even if you don't have it all figured out. Stand in the glow of this awareness, then put your best foot forward on a path that is uniquely your own. Be gentle, be patient, be supportive. Always treat yourself—through words, thoughts, and actions—with the respect you deserve.

Also see 1. Believe, 36. Remember, and 84. Release the (k)nots and Positive Self Talk.

68

Appreciate the journey.

Sometimes, before we can move forward, we need to step back and acknowledge how far we've come. Start by remembering the child you were: perfect in your arrival, present in each moment, and trusting the people around you. Whether or not you received the care and guidance you needed, you were a child finding your way in a new world. Through happy times and sad, habits were formed; some based on the fears and limiting beliefs of others. Skills were acquired: some expressed, some not, some used with less than best intention, while others carried you forward. Consider the lessons and honor it all. Remember to appreciate the qualities that brought you here, such as perseverance, resourcefulness, creativity, and hope. It's all part of your journey. Now, consider the possibility that you're right where you're supposed to be and you have everything you need (like those qualities mentioned earlier) to take the next brilliant step!

For more insight, see 70. Manifest, and 72. Revive.

69

Reconnect with the wonder.

For a morning or a day, disengage from all that is hurtful, negative, cynical, and insensitive. Unplug from all the chatter that you don't want to be true. Skip the news, your email, and social media. Free yourself from what everyone else is doing, thinking, and feeling. Start noticing the wonder around you—from your pets, to your plants, to your own body—and be amazed and thankful for all of their abilities. Go out into your community and be aware of the loving spirit within everyone you see. Smile. Marvel at the buildings, their purpose, and all the people involved in their making and now in their occupying. Imagine the potential! Notice the wildlife, the trees, the light, the shadows, the clouds, the sounds, the scents and all without judgment. Just notice. They all contribute. Bring that sense of awe back into your home and all your relationships. That wonder, that loving essence is always there waiting for us to remember and reconnect.

70

Manifest a childhood dream.

Drift back to earlier times, when you thought about your future and what you wanted to be when you grew up. Did you want to fly to the moon, sail the ocean, work with animals, join the circus, be a teacher, a scientist, or a chef? If you have not yet achieved that early goal, and the thought of it still brings a smile, consider the possibility that your dream can still come true with a little tweaking. A moon flight could be realized by taking up astronomy, buying a telescope to search the stars, creating images of what you might discover along the way, or writing a story about it. Perhaps the flight was really a desire to travel to far away places. Whatever the wish—made a long time ago—you now have the ability to make it happen in some way. And it's possible that the world is waiting. You never know what the path will bring until you decide to follow it. Imagine the possibilities!

71

Learn something new.

Why? **Enrich** an aspect of your life through the knowledge you acquire. **Broaden** your view as you become more aware and willing to explore. **Increase** optimism as you look forward to where your studies will take you. **Boost** your confidence. **Build** a sense of community, especially as you meet new people in that topic. Studies show that new experiences **enhance** your health on multiple levels.

Tips: Be patient. Choose a path that interests you, will benefit you in some way, or simply to energize those brain cells.

Other than local in-person instruction, search online for certificate, degree, or general interest programs. Many have free classes. See Resources: Continuing Education.

72

Revive childlike innocence.

Everything is new to a child. They find absolute delight in the smallest things and expect adventure at every turn. That innocence, that mountain of hope-*full*-ness needs reviving. Remember the simple pleasures: riding your bike, making a new friend, fresh popcorn at the theatre, building sand castles on the beach… Let those memories bring a fresh perspective to the world around you. That potential is still here; you may have simply forgotten how to see. As an adult, you have the resources to revisit the excitement of your childhood or create what you missed. So, swing on a swing, paint purple trees, fly a kite, sing with enthusiasm, build a tree house, ride a skateboard. Capture the joy in the activity you choose, because the more joy you feel—from tiny sparkles to full on fireworks—the more you bring in. Set your sensors to high and welcome child-*ish* bliss!

The delight, the surprise, and the wonder are still here. We just need to remember to look with fresh eyes and be amazed all over again.

73

Promote peace.

Recognize the value in our differences. Discourage jokes or comments that mock or belittle others. Replace criticism with curiosity, and apathy with appreciation. Join a peace-building organization. Start a community or neighborhood group to brainstorm ideas, organize an event, plant a peace garden. Have a neighborhood block party and provide handouts with tips. Bring in a speaker with strategies and activities that encourage communication and harmony. Let your words and actions reflect the peaceful environment you want to see. Be a beacon. Bring peace back to the table, into the mix, off the back burner. Give peace a chance. See Resources: Peace-Building.

Visit KidsforPeaceGlobal.org for a printable peace pledge for your home or office. Read more about them in the Resources: Youth section.

Promise

Continued acts of peace, kindness, and compassion will generate more. That's a promise! It's not just wishful thinking, it's math! But we have to amp it up. Don't wait for someone else to do what feels right to you. You can reach out to a friend, donate to a cause, say thank you, give a compliment, plant a flower, raise a peace flag, smile at a stranger, leave a thoughtful note, and so much more. It only takes a minute!

74

Contact your legislators.

Since our representatives work for us, we have a reasonable right to be heard. How? Call their office (most effective), write a letter (handwritten gets more attention), or send an e-mail. Also, submit testimony on bills you believe in. Track their status by entering *bill tracking* as an Internet search term or on USA.gov. For contact information, visit your state's website or search the Internet with *how to contact your legislator* for more tips. Will it make a difference? It won't if you don't!

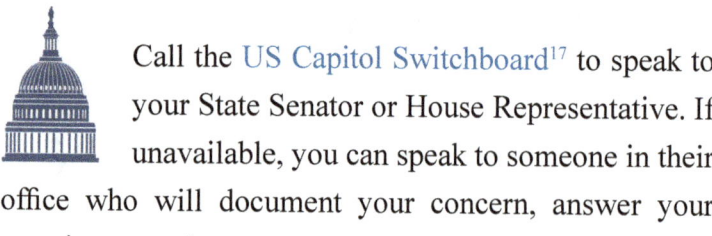

Call the US Capitol Switchboard[17] to speak to your State Senator or House Representative. If unavailable, you can speak to someone in their office who will document your concern, answer your questions, or take a message.   202-224-3121

---

[17] The Capitol Switchboard is a referral number only. It is not listed in Resources.

75

Get involved in the legal system.

If you are interested in the law—its interpretation and enforcement—bring your ideas to the legal community by joining a committee, focus or advocacy group. Visit a law library. Call an attorney working in a field that interests you. Many legal, justice, and advocacy organizations appreciate volunteers with or without legal experience. Check their websites for *Volunteer* or *Get Involved* sections. Network with change-makers until you find a group that's right for you. You may find that the group you're looking for doesn't exist. Start one!

To locate a legal aid office, visit LSC.gov and click on the *Get Legal Help* button to access their search tool.

76

Participate in the political process.

Attend town hall or local council meetings. Work on a campaign. Run for office. Volunteer for local elections. Vote! Remind friends, family, and co-workers to vote. Join a political organization. Contact current or former local politicians for suggestions on how to get involved. Volunteer at organizations that benefit the community. Take a class in politics, history, equality, or public service and meet others that share your interest.

Direct your energy and political passion where it can do some good! See 4. Community, and 92. Gather.

77

Increase joy. Decrease violence.

It seems simplistic to suggest that if we turn up the joy, we'll turn down the violence, but it's true. Violence is a reflection of fear, and in a fearful environment there is little joy. To decrease the violence, we stop tolerating it by being aware of its presence, its triggers, and how it enters our space. Is it a lack of rules, communication, or mutual respect? Does it come from people, games, movies, music, news, or social media? Whatever the source, learn how to stop the flow, because a lack of response to violence suggests that it's normal, acceptable, and inevitable. It is not. Shift your awareness! Start choosing life-affirming thoughts and actions until joy is overflowing. Prepare, insist, and invite activities, conversation, and behavior to foster greater harmony. Choose joy!

78

Rethink, redefine, recycle.

It's more than bottles and cans. It's a social movement to rethink how we treat the things in our lives from products to people to the environment. It's a concept of greater awareness that demonstrates thoughtfulness, creativity, and a general regard for others—past, present, and future. Simple mindful actions from re-gifting to restoring can re-energize industries, brighten our communities, and uplift our families. It's about second chances and new life. Renew, reassign, recreate, reorganize, redesign, replant, rebuild…

Learn how others **around the world** are rethinking their place and their impact. Turn to the Resources section for a short list of Positive News & Inspiring Video sites.

79

Model the behavior you want to see.

We all learn by example. Consider the actions you have witnessed that touched your heart. Maybe it was a passing kindness between strangers, an elderly couple holding hands, or a random compliment in the market. Maybe it was in the smile that crossed a friend's face in hearing a caring voice on the other end of the phone, or in the person sitting across from you who took the time to listen to your concern or delight in your good news. Whether it's with food, through language, in exercise, attention, education, work, play, people, or pets, explore the wholesome behavior you value and be a shining example of that.

Be
a beacon.
Be a role
model of
kindness,
health,
calm,
patience,
enthusiasm,
joy…

Shine a light
for us
to
follow!

Thailand

80

Explore the true meaning of love.

This is a definition you need to understand for yourself. In your search you will find a lot of statements about what love is not and hear about the pain it causes. But, truly, meditate on this. How does it feel? What does it look like? Is it visible in our environment or only between people? The more you think about it, the more you may find that you can not quite describe it in words, yet deep down you know it well. Make a list of what you love. Use your list to lift you when you are down or to remind you of the love in your life.

For more context, see 48. Do more, 81. *Love* never hurts, and 101. Love more.

81

Know that *Love* never hurts.

We use the word a lot. We love food, that song, that car... It's a way to show our passion and delight, and that's a good thing. But sometimes love gets confused with pain. There are plenty of lyrics and movies about how love hurts, but, really, it doesn't. Sure it hurts to love someone who doesn't love us back but it's not love that's causing the pain; it's the absence of it. Our resistance—through lack, disconnection, or a belief in how others define love—is what hurts. Love is pure, uncluttered, and limitless. Love, in and of itself, cannot hurt. Love comforts. Love inspires. Love is everywhere.

See 101. Love more.

82

Be curious.

A competitive, cynical, and negative environment might steer our attention to our differences as a form of protection. But to bridge differences, we have to engage our curiosity, especially if we feel the urge to criticize or judge. Instead, ask a genuine *why* or *what makes you say that or feel that way*, and wait for the answer with an open mind. It's not about being right or wrong, it's just a nonjudgmental wondering about another point of view. Curiosity, if we let it, can lead us on a path of discovery we might not have imagined before.

Ask more questions and gain a new perspective that could enrich all your relationships.

83

Turn conflict into a shared accomplishment.

A conflict can lead to a standstill or a breakthrough. The difference depends on intention and attitude. If we are more invested in winning, being right, or shutting down the opposite view, we miss the opportunity for expansion. Next time you notice signs of tension or resistance, engage methods to keep the conversation going in an atmosphere of cooperation. Identify a common goal. Agree to work together and resolve amicably. Identify the facts, listen carefully, ask questions, and explore alternatives. There are strategies that work! Study mediation, take a class, or attend a lecture. For insight, search GreaterGood.berkeley.edu. for related articles.

84

Release the (k)nots.

Have you gotten into a habit of saying can't, won't, shouldn't, couldn't, not now, not good enough, not smart enough, not enough time? Release the *nots*! Change your language to reflect what you <u>can</u> do and appreciate <u>now</u>. When you do, you open to a field of possibilities.

Why? If you focus on only what you're trying to avoid, don't like, and don't want, there is not much room for wonder, joy, and abundance. And, that habit of nots is creating tension and stress in your body, so it's likely that when you release the nots, some other knots will go too. Aaahhh!

Positive Self Talk

Do you have an inner dialogue that is often negative and worrisome? This pattern may have become a habit. The good news? You can change it! Start by noticing when a negative thought pops up and replace it with a positive one. This will take some perspective and practice, but it's well worth the effort! The more encouraging and supportive your inner dialogue, the more your outer world can reflect the positive messages you affirm.

Discover the power of words by searching for articles and books on *positive self talk*.[18] For more insight, see 87. Cultivate.

---

[18] Also see Further Reading for book titles *You Can Heal Your Life* by Louise Hay and *Every Word Has Power* by Yvonne Oswald.

85

Care more.

Contrary to some societal messaging, emotional awareness and expression is a strength that has the potential to enhance any connection and enable us to live more fully. So, by all means, use your words, but also remember to do something that shows you care. Active listening, healthy touch, eye contact, being inclusive, and asking questions while respecting boundaries and comfort levels are just a few ways of showing genuine interest. Don't stop the impulse to share positive emotions in words, actions, decisions, projects, and relationships at work, home, or in public. Let that spirit guide you. You may not always get the reaction you want, because others are dealing with their stuff, but don't stop; just stop the expectation. Find new avenues to share. In the process, you will find that others care, too, and through that interaction a kindness wave will be generated.

86

Forgive yourself.

Who wants to be stuck in the past? But that's what happens when we hold onto the pain from our choices or those of others. We cannot change what happened, but we can change our understanding and attitude about it. Release the guilt and shame by accepting responsibility for your actions, intentional or not, by identifying what motivated you. It's possible that you (or they) did what was best with what was known at the time. Regardless, that was then. A fresh start requires recognition, acceptance, and forward movement. When you're ready, stop being angry or disappointed, stop allowing the hurt to continue, and free that energy to receive from the abundance this life has to offer. It really is a choice: pain or joy? While you're at it, fill that new space with self-esteem, trust, and encouragement so you don't slide back into an old pattern. Full speed ahead, my friend!

If your thoughts create
your future, what will
you think about today
and where will that take
you tomorrow?

Deutschland

87

Cultivate a positive outlook.

There is sound research on the influence a positive mindset has on relationships, health, and achievement. Yet, we are often bombarded with bad news, speculation, and criticism. Too much gloom, doom, and doubt can skew our perception to a point where all we see is what has or could go wrong. Although we want to feel prepared and protected, we have to maintain some balance and that requires a shift in perspective. For example, while a job loss can feel devastating, it can also provide an opportunity to use our talents, develop new skills, and be more fulfilled. So turn away from too much negative input and increase your circle of positive people and activities. This isn't about ignoring negative emotions. It's about reconciling those that repeat, so you can refocus on the peace, love, and joy that is your birthright.

Also see 88. Smile, 95. Abundance, and 96. Miracles. Looking for more? Check Resources: Positive News & Inspiring Video.

88

Smile more.

Even when you don't feel like it, pushing a smile onto your face can signal the release of feel-good chemicals.[19] You may feel silly, but that silliness can encourage tension to fade and make room for ease and inspiration to flow. Smile by admitting you've gotten yourself into a crazy situation. Smile at any challenge knowing you will get through it and your frowns will flip more frequently. Create a *smile file* filled with images of happy faces, places, quotes—anything that brings you joy. Smile at someone. Their smile back will make yours more genuine as some frustration, disappointment, and sadness releases. Smile because there is always something to smile about.

Bonus! Reduce stress, elevate mood, lower blood pressure, reduce pain. Sound familiar? See 6. Mindful and 49. Nature. There's a trend! Imagine a mindful walk in nature with a smile on your face. WOW!

---

[19] Stibich, "10 Big Benefits."

89

Begin each day knowing you make a difference.

Sometimes we may feel insignificant and wonder if we make a difference at all. Truth is, and whether we realize it or not, we have an effect on the world around us. And with intention and focus, we can feel a whole lot better about the marks we leave behind. We may not see the results or get feedback, but keep going. You absolutely do matter and more than you know.

How? Start each day visualizing favorable results and let those images guide your actions. Be aware of your talk to yourself and others, and replace words of criticism with caring and gratitude. Write an affirmation or intention for the day based on what you want to embody, such as: confidence, creativity, trust, joy. Know that your positive vibes are having a positive effect. Let your goodness shine! It's a gift that keeps on giving.

90

Get moving!

Feeling stuck? That's when it's time to get moving—physically—to circulate that blocked energy. And it helps to do that outside.

Why? Because when you're all caught up in the negative, you're looking back and not forward. Fresh air, sunshine, open space, more people and wildlife will help you see your situation differently as you become more aware of the options out there. Go for a walk or a swim, do some stretches, shake off the bad vibes, ride a bike, stomp your feet. Release all that stuck energy so you can do what's important to you. Move that energy physically, emotionally, intellectually, and spiritually. It's like clogged pipes. Once you clear the debris, the water can flow. Start moving with the intention of breaking free from whatever is holding you back. Move that energy in the direction you want to go! See the Quick Release after Way #13. Step away.

91

Focus on peace. Focus on compassion.

It's easy to get caught up in a problem, what's missing in our life, or the fear of either. But too much attention on what we don't want, seems only to attract more of the same. Next time, try to catch yourself when this thought pattern strikes. Stop the chatter and redirect your attention to the peaceful interactions you want to see. When peace is our focus, we are far more likely to create opportunities that define it, such as inclusion, cooperation, creative expression, and harmony. It's the same with compassion. By deliberately choosing to be more understanding and acknowledging the feelings and kind acts of others, the more compassion we'll find. Peace and compassion are always present. It's simply a matter of choosing on their behalf.

92

Gather for a common cause.

Consider joining or starting a group with a common interest, such as literature, crafts, hiking, astronomy, photography. Maybe you want to be more involved in community projects. Search for or start a group that meets regularly to identify and resolve local, national, or global issues, or support those organizations that do. Be sure to choose one that truly aligns with your interests, beliefs, and concerns.

You are not alone. Many, like you, just need a nudge. Reach out to others of like-mind and be amazed at the powers of connection. Ask among your friends, coworkers, and colleagues. Contact your local librarian for general or specific topic resources.

93

Promote equality, inclusion, and cooperation.

Imagine the potential in all of humanity when we cherish each other's ideas, opinions, and feelings. Imagine feeling free to explore and express what is important to us. For too long, a patriarchal system has dominated half the global population—the feminine—treating them as less than the other half simply because of their sex. This dynamic has also caused other populations to be silenced, minimized, and oppressed. Imagine the wisdom, truth, and creativity that has been lost over the centuries!

A transition is taking place. So stand tall. Get involved. Be authentic. Use your words, your talent, and intention in a spirit of equality, compassion, and freedom.

Visit Resources: Equality, Partnership, Women for groundbreaking, mind-expanding, ongoing work in these fields. There is much we can do!

Equality in Action

We can all be more aware of our social footprint—the marks we leave on our world—by making more mindful, appreciative, responsible, and empowering choices that honor everyone.

Language—the words we use and those we don't.

Media—programs we watch, music we listen to, and social media activity we support either passively or intentionally.

Behavior—the way we treat others, the respect and appreciation we show, our engagement in the world around us.

The next time you feel the urge to hold back, bite your tongue, settle for less, feel "they" must know better, or think no one will listen or care,

Canada

remember the commitment of so many that came before you, are here now, and are yet to come. Celebrate their spirit and honor their courage by using your voice now.

94

Renew your spirit.

This is on you, because you're the one that knows what makes you feel vibrant, valuable, and fulfilled. Remember who you are on a deeper level—underneath all the *shoulds*, *coulds*, and *have to's*—and reconnect. Not sure how to proceed? Start fresh. List all that you find enriching, encouraging, inspiring, and calming. What brings *you* back into alignment? If you have discovered what gives your life meaning and purpose, include those elements on your list. Merge those activities back into your life and awaken a power and wholeness that you may have thought was lost. Reconsider those nagging thoughts—the ones that keep reminding you to do that something you know will make you smile.

Feel Good Journal

Fill a journal or photo binder with your favorite uplifting quotations, pep talks, positive memories, or trinkets you've saved that warm your heart or make you laugh. Include words and images that remind you of your strength, ability, and destiny—that thing you know you are meant to do.

Include affirmations that promote self-confidence and well-being. Examples:
I am patient, kind, and understanding.
I make decisions with ease and clarity.
I am a lovable and worthwhile person.

They may not feel true in a moment of tension, but they have likely been true before. Repeating it can help you feel more in control and certainly more optimistic. Be sure to choose words that have meaning for you and reflect the outcome you are trying to achieve. While you're at it, frame some of those quotes and images and put them up where you can see them often.

95

Delight in the abundance.

Every day a life is saved, a spirit is lifted, a habit is broken, a life-affirming decision is made, someone is helped anonymously, money/material/time is donated to a cause, advances are made to a cure, someone is healed, a revelation occurs, a seed is planted, a friendship endures, a love deepens, a flower blooms, a risk becomes a blessing, the impossible occurs.

Good things happen all the time and every where. Pay attention. Seek them out. They are in abundance.

96

Expect miracles.

This is about trust, a deep sense of knowing, and letting go. By expecting miracles we choose to believe that something considered impossible or unknown can become a reality. We may not know how, when, or why—and that may not be important—but we can simply direct our energy into the possibility and let go of the worry. It's a happy thought! After all, decisions are being made, attitudes are shifting, and ideas are emerging with the capability of changing what once could not be done. Anything can happen and it might be happening right now! Optimism clears the mind for new adventures. Be open, be patient, and step into the ever-present flow of possibilities with trust and appreciation.

97

Make wishes.

Because we should always have hope. It's okay to want, to dream, and to expect because that is how we tap into our authentic nature—our true selves—and we need more truthful expression. Wishes are like guide posts clarifying intention and focusing energy in a specific direction. Make a wish and release it into the universe. Every reality started with a thought, an idea, the possibility of what could be. A wish provides a light to follow reflecting what is in your heart.

98

Be part of the solution.

Whether you do something on your own or choose to be part of a larger group, the goal is to actively participate in creating a more loving and healthy environment for everyone. Every problem has a solution. Your voice might provide the perspective and be a catalyst for real problem-solving to occur. Step up, join in, and be part of a movement to increase harmony across the planet. Review this list of *101 Ways* and mark those that resonate with you. Add them to your routine and be like a candle that lights the room and lights the way.

99

Share this list.

Drop one on a co-worker's desk or post it on a bulletin board. Share with a teacher to discuss with her students. Send one to a friend. Frame it for display in your home or office. Ask a local business, community center, or library to position one in their window. Start a study group to discuss it or an action committee to implement it. Visit Inspired101.com[20] for a printable list of *101 Ways to Wow! Our World.*

---

[20] Inspired101.com currently redirects to DebbieJenae.com. Neither site has a separate listing in the Resources section.

100

Create your own list.

This list is not all-inclusive. Consider the possible solutions unique to your situation, your neighborhood, or with someone you know. Write down those actions you believe will have the best overall results. Post it where you can see it or others can add to it. Flag one for the focus of the day. Above all, take action!

101

Love more.

Love is our essence. It resides in each and every one of us waiting to be released, shared, expressed, and experienced in its fullness. It inspires us to be true and, like the air we breathe and the space we inhabit, it connects us to everything. Love is everywhere, in all ways, and all the time. It can ease a frantic pace into a gentle rhythm of appreciation or direct it with passion and possibility. It arrives in a wave of joy or in the silence of curiosity and understanding. It is an energy that is magical in its grace, intention, and abundance.

Love is patient, kind, encouraging, nurturing, and healing. It can take your breath away, put you at a loss for words, completely surprise you, and slowly *inner*whelm you. When all is said and done, *Love* is all there is, all you are, and all that matters.

Love a whole lot more.[21]

---
[21] Jenae, *Your Light, Your Life!*

By Category

About Categories

The List is separated into six categories. A number identifies its position on the 2-page spread near the front of this book and in the *101 Ways* section that follows.

You will notice that some of the *101 Ways* could easily appear in multiple categories. That is the beauty of *the List*—versatility.

- Taking care of yourself
- If you or someone you know needs help
- Relating to children
- In your community
- Habits worth keeping
- Things to think about

Taking care of yourself

Believe in your potential. [1]

Maintain a daily practice of mindful awareness. [6]

Discover your sacred space. [26]

Take a communication class. [35]

Resolve old beliefs around power, intimacy, and control. [40]

Do more of what you love. [48]

Trust more. [58]

Define and defend what is right and true for you. [62]

Receive graciously. [63]

Treat yourself with the respect you deserve. [67]

Appreciate the journey. [68]

Reconnect with the wonder. [69]

Manifest a childhood dream. [70]

Learn something new. [71]

Revive childlike innocence. [72]

Forgive yourself. [86]

Begin each day knowing you make a difference. [89]

If you or someone you know needs help

Feel you're losing it? …Go for a walk. 7

…Take a bath. 8

…Count to 10, slowly. 9

…Call a friend. 10

…Call a hotline. 11

…Stop. Take 3 slow, deep breaths. Repeat. 12

…Step away. 13

Take a break. Don't break someone's spirit. 14

Tell someone. Report suspected abuse. 17

Have integrity. Say what you mean, do what you say. 18

Make it safe to share feelings and ideas. 38

Take an *alternatives to violence* class. 41

Know that asking for help takes courage and demonstrates strength. 42

Heal your wounds. Know you can. 43

Accept the help you deserve. 44

Share your wisdom. 45

Relating to children

Talk and listen to children. 2

Speak up for a child. 15

Spare the rod; love the child. 16

Protect all children. 19

Give praise. 20

Be honest with children. 22

Make time for the children in your life. 28

Read to a child. 29

Embrace each stage of a child's development. 30

Respect the rights of every child. 32

Enhance your child caring and awareness skills. 34

Engage in healthy play. 47

Create family traditions to cherish. 57

Make mealtime a special time to nourish and connect. 59

Teach rather than control. 60

Be the parent you wish you had. 66

See children as a gift, yourself as their guide. 65

In your community

Radiate respect. 3
Get involved in your community. 4
Empower victims of domestic violence. 23
Donate the cost of a counseling session. 24
Gift your time, services, money to a vision you support. 25
Connect with a mentoring program. 31
Demonstrate responsibility. 33
Share your talents. 37
Be an inspiration! 55
Honor the boundaries of others. 61
Contact your legislators. 74
Get involved in the legal system. 75
Participate in the political process. 76
Rethink, redefine, recycle. 78
Model the behavior you want to see. 79
Gather for a common cause. 92
Share this list. 99

Habits worth keeping

Join the kindness movement. 27

Choose your words with care. 46

Spend time in nature. 49

Be kind to animals. 50

Support, encourage, and preserve creative expression. 51

Extend courtesy. 56

Say thank you. 64

Promote peace. 73

Increase joy. Decrease violence. 77

Be curious. 82

Care more. 85

Cultivate a positive outlook. 87

Smile more. 88

Focus on peace. Focus on compassion. 91

Promote equality, inclusion, and cooperation. 93

Renew your spirit. 94

Be part of the solution. 98

Things to think about

Honor the spirit in others. 5

See a mistake as an opportunity. 21

Remember your magnificence. 36

Let fear be a nudge, not an anchor. 39

Celebrate your efforts. 52

Speak the truth. 53

Ask: What is the loving thing to do? 54

Explore the true meaning of love. 80

Know that *Love* never hurts. 81

Turn conflict into a shared accomplishment. 83

Release the (k)nots. 84

Get moving! 90

Delight in the abundance. 95

Expect miracles. 96

Make wishes. 97

Create your own list. 100

Love more. 101

Reach Out

For Parents and Caregivers

- Know where your children are.

- Make sure those in your care memorize your full name, address, and phone number. It's not enough to have this important information written down or in their cell phone. They should know it by heart.

- Teach them about calling 911. (See that listing under Resources: CALL)

- Create an emergency plan to include:
  - How unscheduled pickups will be handled
  - Trusted adults to contact for help
  - A code word or signal to use, if necessary

- Notice and respond appropriately to drastic changes in:
  - Behavior
  - Reactions to others
  - Appearance

- Be a trustworthy adult with your words, actions, and responses. (For lots of parent and relationship tips, see Resources: Healthy Mind, Body, Spirit; and Parents & Caregivers.)

About Reporting

If you know a child or adult is being abused or in immediate danger, call 911. If you *suspect* the same, contact an appropriate agency for information, guidance, or referral. See Resources: CALL and FIND. Also know:

- As part of a report, the agency may ask you a series of questions. **Your answers** will help them provide the best response by knowing as much as possible about the situation as you see it.

- If you are concerned about someone's safety (friend, neighbor, relative, child), call their local police and request a **Police Welfare Check** (see *Way* #17. Tell Someone).

Children

- **State laws vary**. To learn more, contact your local child protection agency, visit your local law library, or explore the *Resources* at ChildWelfare.gov.

- You can and should **ask questions** about the reporting process. Call, or check the local child protection agency website for details. Search for *child protection* in *your state* or call USA.gov

- All states have laws about who is required (**mandated reporters**) to report suspected child abuse. Some examples are teachers, health care workers, law enforcement, and childcare providers.

- You can **report anonymously**. Child welfare agencies and law enforcement are generally required to keep your information confidential.

- The person you name in a report is **not entitled** to know who made the report.

- A report of child abuse does not automatically result in the **child's removal** from the home.

Your call may save a life, stop further abuse, and start a healing process.

Counseling

It can be difficult to confide in others, to admit that we are faced with a situation that feels bigger than us or one we might not be able to handle alone. And sometimes we just want another view, some feedback, or emotional support. Even if you have to pay someone to listen, you deserve to be heard and understood, and you are worth the time and attention it takes to heal the wounds that have been created along the way, regardless of the cause. An unresolved issue can be like having a locked room in your home that you never use—space you cannot transform and enjoy because you don't want to look. Accept your current situation, regardless of how you got there, then summon your courage. It's in there, waiting.

Finding a Counselor

Do your homework. You want a partner to your well-being; someone who can help you be you again; someone who believes in your value and your potential.

Common Concerns

Connect with a counselor or group with a focus on your particular concern, such as relationships, alcohol or drugs, childhood abuse, depression, anger, parenting, or grief. Maybe you just feel a bit lost or disconnected. Mention this to the counselor in your introductory contact.

Personal Referral

The best source is through those that you trust. Consider starting with a friend, neighbor, relative, co-worker, or medical professional.

Employment

Your employer's human resources department may have a list of referrals or partner with local agencies that offer discounted rates.

Internet

Visit NetworkTherapy.com, a searchable directory for locating a counselor in your area (see Resources: FIND), or enter *finding a counselor* as an Internet search term.

Contact

Now that you have some names, make a list of general questions to ask when you call. Notice how the staff responds to you. Interview the counselors over the phone or in person and see how comfortable you would feel talking with them further. They should be willing to answer your questions and it's important that you ask.

- Did they seem sincere, compassionate, and knowledgeable?

- Did they answer your questions about qualifications, fees, and insurance?

- How about scheduling, length of visits, individual or group counseling?

- What about their philosophy on treatment and healing in general?

If not, keep looking. There are plenty of good counselors out there, and you deserve a match that is in your best interests, which includes:

- Communication styles
- Personality
- Experience
- Openness

By the way, once you find one, know that it's okay to change between group and individual counseling, or change programs altogether as long as you know you're not running away. It's okay to take a break; it's okay to start fresh. Trust your inner guidance to know what's best for you at any given time. See the Resources: CALL and FIND sections to get started.

Resources

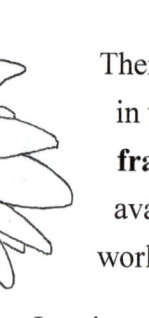

There are 84 resources in this section—a **fraction** of what's available in the world.

I reviewed those I was familiar with, drawn to, or that appeared on my **radar**. Use *your* radar to find what's right for you.

If nothing else, browse through these pages in **awe**, because there are a lot of people here and a lot more out there doing remarkably loving, helpful, and exciting work.

About Resources

- All are provided to give you a place to start or help you find one in your community, state, or country.

- Most have easily accessible information you can use now.

- Most are based in the United States, some are outside, and others work internationally.

- Descriptions were verified and approved with each organization, except for some government sites. That information was found on their website, often on the *About Us* page.

- Check their *Resources*, *Sponsor*, or *Partner* pages for links to other organizations.

- Websites change. If the content has moved, contact the site or use their search tool to locate the document, article, title, or topic. An Internet search may also bring up helpful results.

- Some resources could easily be listed under multiple categories. Check through them all and flag those that resonate with you.

Resources

CALL for Help, Support, Referral, or Information

The terms *hotline* and *helpline* are often used interchangeably, but their services differ. Hotlines, or crisis lines, address more urgent needs on a particular topic; some may activate emergency services. *Helplines* offer callers support, information, and other resources.

- Always ask questions when you call any "line" or check their website to make sure they provide the help or service you need.

- Hotlines are typically staffed 24 hours a day, 7 days a week (24/7).

- Many lines have language translation services, text, and chat capability. Ask or check the website.

- Resources in other sections may have links to other hotline or helpline listings.

- *Toll-free* phone numbers used in this book (begin with 800, 844, 866, 877, or 888) are free to use in the US from a landline. Check your provider or cellular plan to see if rates apply.

Emergency Assistance & Reporting

911 is the national emergency number to call in the US and Canada if you or someone else is hurt, in danger, or in immediate need of police, fire, or medical assistance. Not sure if it's an emergency? Call 911 and let them decide. Visit the NENA website to learn more. Check the *Advocacy, Stats, & FAQ* tab for "Tips for Callers," and the *Standards* tab for *Public Education Tools* to locate the "Making 9-1-1 Work for YOU! E-Brochure" for shareable, age appropriate, printable information for your family, friends, and community. Available 24/7.
911　　　　　　　　　　　　　　　　　　nena.org

Hotlines & Helplines

988 SUICIDE & CRISIS LIFELINE is a national network of trained counselors that provide life-saving crisis support and resources to people in suicidal crisis or emotional distress. In the US call, text, or chat for yourself or someone you care about. Visit their site for more. Available 24/7, 365 days a year.
988　　　　　　　　　　　　　　　　988lifeline.org

Not in a crisis, but want to talk to someone? See Warmlines under FIND a Helping Resource.

Resources

BOYS TOWN NATIONAL HOTLINE is a crisis, resource, and referral number for kids, teens, and parents —male or female, no matter the issue. Some reasons to call: relationship issues, depression, suicide, abuse, addiction, anger, or school problems. Available 24/7.
800-448-3000 boystown.org/hotline

CHILDHELP NATIONAL CHILD ABUSE HOTLINE is dedicated to the prevention of child abuse. Serving the US and Canada, professional crisis counselors offer crisis intervention, information, and referrals to emergency, social service, and support resources. Check their site for more. Available 24/7.
800-422-4453 (1-800-4-A-CHILD) childhelphotline.org

LOVE IS RESPECT offers information, support, and advocacy to young people ages 13 to 26 with questions about their romantic relationships. (Also see Youth.)
866-331-9474 loveisrespect.org

NATIONAL DOMESTIC VIOLENCE HOTLINE brings support, crisis intervention information, education, and referral services in over 200 languages to help survivors of domestic violence live free of abuse. The Hotline's advocates are available via phone, chat, and text to help everyone affected by abuse. Visit their *Get Help* section to create a *Safety Plan* and more. Available 24/7.
800-799-SAFE (7233) thehotline.org

CALL

NATIONAL HUMAN TRAFFICKING HOTLINE connects victims and survivors of sex and labor trafficking with services and supports to get help and stay safe. If you or someone you know is experiencing human trafficking and in need of support, call this Hotline. You can also learn more about trafficking, get safety planning tips, and find local services by visiting their site. All calls are confidential. Hotline operates 24/7.
888-373-7888   humantraffickinghotline.org

If you suspect a child or adult is being abused or in immediate danger, call 911.

If the danger is not immediate, and you want to know more about what you can do, call local police or a related number—such as those in this CALL section—to be connected or referred.

Information only

CDC-INFO is the Centers for Disease Control and Prevention line with live agents trained to search CDC resources to help you find the latest reliable science-based general health information. Agents do not diagnose or provide medical advice. (Also see CDC main listing under Healthy Mind, Body, Spirit.) Limited hours.
800-CDC-INFO (800-232-4636)   cdc.gov/cdc-info

Resources

FIND a Helping Resource

CHILD HELPLINE INTERNATIONAL is a global network of child helplines that shares research, data, and experiences to ensure that children have access to high-quality child helpline services. Find a child helpline in your country.   childhelplineinternational.org

ELDERCARE LOCATOR connects older Americans and their caregivers with local support resources. Common needs include meals, home care or transportation, caregiver training or a well-deserved break from caregiving responsibilities. Call, or search their site by city, state, zip, or county.
800-677-1116 Limited hours.   eldercare.acl.gov

LEGAL SERVICES CORPORATION has a searchable directory of legal aid offices that they fund to provide civil legal services to low income Americans. Call or access the directory through their site. (Full listing under Legal.)
202-295-1500   lsc.gov

NETWORKTHERAPY.COM has a directory of mental health providers in the US and Canada. Check their *Resource Center* for hotlines and support groups. (Also under Healthy Mind, Body, Spirit.)   networktherapy.com

OFFICE FOR VICTIMS OF CRIME is committed to enhancing the Nation's capacity to assist crime victims and provide leadership in changing attitudes, policies, and practices to promote justice and healing for all victims of crime. Visit the *Help for Victims* page to access a list of *Toll Free, Text, and Online Hotlines*, to find help in *Your State*, and other services. ovc.ojp.gov

USA.GOV is the official website of the US Government. Their mission is to make it easier for people to find and understand government services and information. Includes a *Directory of US Government Agencies and Departments*. Call, or visit their site to find your topic or use their search tool. You could be three clicks away from the answer you've been looking for!
844-USA-GOV1 (1-844-872-4681) Limited hours.
usa.gov

US DEPARTMENT OF HEALTH AND HUMAN SERVICES administers more than 100 programs to protect and enhance the health and well-being of all Americans. Check their *Programs & Services* tab for topics that interest you. Locate the *HHS FAQs* link (bottom of page) for common questions and to enter a search term. Lots of information here!
877-696-6775 Limited hours. hhs.gov

Warmlines

Warmlines are for callers who may not be in crisis but are still seeking some level of support. The intention is to reduce hospitalizations and forced treatment by providing help before it reaches a crisis. Warmlines are generally staffed by trained peer specialists who listen, offer ideas and hope based on their own experience in recovery. Search the Internet for warmlines in your country.

WARMLINE DIRECTORY lists all the known warmlines around the US—currently more than 100!—with helpful information about each one. They also work to provide a community among caregivers and support among warmline staff. Find a warmline that works for you, and learn more about the why, research, surveys, and training via this site. warmline.org

The Arts

Arts programs benefit everyone. Check your community college and university extension programs for classes. Have an idea or want to get involved? Try your local Chamber of Commerce, Rotary Club, or City Council for community projects and committees to bring the arts to your neighborhood. Search the Internet for *arts in (your state)* or *arts councils*. The following organizations may provide more insight, encouragement, and ideas.

AMERICANS FOR THE ARTS is a nonprofit advancing the extraordinary and dynamic value of arts and culture by empowering local arts agencies to make arts and culture essential to community vitality. There's lots to explore for advocates, artists, researchers, and leaders. Some *Topics* include *Arts in Business, Education,* and *Healing.* On the home page, click *LAA Wayfinder* for a living directory of local arts agencies, and the *Job Bank* for opportunities. americansforthearts.org

NATIONAL ASSEMBLY OF STATE ARTS AGENCIES is dedicated to strengthening the nation's 56 state and jurisdictional arts agencies to ensure that every community in America receives the cultural, civic, economic, and educational benefits of the arts. Access NASAA's *State Arts Agency Directory* to locate the agency with grants, programs, and opportunities in your state. nasaa-arts.org

NATIONAL ENDOWMENT FOR THE ARTS (NEA) is an independent federal agency established by Congress in 1965 that recognizes the arts continuing contribution to the well-being of individuals, communities, and local economies. The NEA is the largest funder of the arts and arts education in communities nationwide. Explore the *Grant Announcements* in previous years and the *Impact* section for samples of NEA-funded projects in your state or region. You may find a surprising way to get involved or the motivation to pursue your own arts idea. arts.gov

Resources

Continuing Education

Want to further your career, follow a new interest, or share your expertise? Here are 4 online options to explore.

COURSERA partners with more than 325 leading universities and companies to bring flexible, affordable, job-relevant topics to individuals and organizations worldwide. Some courses are free! coursera.org

OPENLEARN is the free learning platform of The Open University, delivered as part of its Royal Charter and its commitment to delivering exceptional open education to learners across the world. openlearn.com

THE GREAT COURSES PLUS offers learning from award-winning experts and professors from the most respected institutions in the world. Occasional discounts up to 70% once a year. See what's available!
800-832-2412 thegreatcoursesplus.com

UDEMY transforms lives through learning by ensuring everyone has access to the latest and most relevant skills. The platform offers thousands of courses in dozens of languages, some fee-based and some at no cost. Become an instructor on Udemy and inspire others! udemy.com

Empowering Survivors of Abuse

A survivor's experience, knowledge, and perspective is critically important to preventing abuse in the future. Let's listen and learn. When we empower survivors, we empower the world! Not a survivor of abuse? Share the caring and respect you experienced and provide active examples for what healthy relationships are all about.

ASCA program for adult survivors of child abuse is the free "Survivor to Thriver" manual with 21 self-help steps to healing and recovery. The program's ASCA peer-led support groups offer emotional support and validation; an opportunity to express feelings, thoughts, memories, hopes, and insights; and education on the subject of child abuse. ascasupport.org

BLUE KNOT is an Australia based foundation that advocates for and provides support to anyone affected by complex trauma, including those who support them, personally and professionally. Examples of complex trauma include violence, abuse, neglect or exploitation experienced as a child, young person or adult. Click through their *Survivors*, *Supporters*, and *Resources* sections for lots of helpful reading. blueknot.org.au

Resources

CANADIAN WOMEN'S FOUNDATION created the *Signal for Help* (see #17. Tell) as a simple one-handed gesture to silently communicate a need for help. Visit their site for an action guide and free mini-course for *Signal For Help Responders*. Also see their work in support of gender justice and equality.   canadianwomen.org

DOMESTICSHELTERS.ORG has lots of helpful tools and information on various topics for people experiencing–, at risk of–, and working to end domestic violence. A searchable directory of domestic violence programs and shelters in the US and Canada makes it easier to find services best suited to victims and their supporters.   domesticshelters.org

HELP FOR ADULT VICTIMS OF CHILD ABUSE is based in the United Kingdom run by volunteers dedicated to provide support, friendship and advice for adults who have been affected by childhood abuse. They have an online *Survivor's Forum* and a treasure of information and resources on issues affecting survivors.   havoca.org

SURVIVORS.ORG is a database tool to make it easier for trauma survivors to take control of their holistic healing and find the resources they need to thrive. Resources include rape crisis centers, therapy, legal assistance, groups, healing, medical, and safety. Search by keyword, location, or category.   survivors.org

Equality • Partnership • Women

More resources are becoming available as we shift and transform old beliefs to create a harmonious balance of feminine and masculine energies across the planet. Here are a few that focus on partnership, equality, masculinity, and women's rights and history.

CENTER FOR PARTNERSHIP SYSTEMS (CPS) provides a roadmap to a new world based on partnership rather than domination. Founded by Riane Eisler, the Center's programs focus on human rights and nonviolence, gender and racial equity, child development, and a new Social Wealth Index that values the financial contribution of the work of caring for people and nature. Click *Programs* to access the free "Caring and Connected Parenting: A Guide to Raising Connected Children," and *Take Action* for so much more.   centerforpartnership.org

EQUALRIGHTSAMENDMENT.ORG is hosted by the Alice Paul (ERA author and women's suffrage leader) Center for Gender Justice, an organization that advocates for ratification of the ERA. An equal rights amendment to the US Constitution was first introduced in 1923 and, as of July 2025, these rights are still not secure. Learn why it's important, the history, status, what you can do, other links, and more.   equalrightsamendment.org

EQUIMUNDO: CENTER FOR MASCULINITIES AND SOCIAL JUSTICE works to transform intergenerational patterns of harm and promote patterns of care, empathy, and accountability among boys and men. Resources include program manuals, learning briefs, and reports. Be sure to check out the most recent versions of "State of the World's Fathers" and "State of American Men."

equimundo.org

NATIONAL ORGANIZATION FOR MEN AGAINST SEXISM is a pro-feminist, LGBTQ+ affirmative, anti-racist, anti-classist organization dedicated to enhancing men's lives and committed to justice on social issues including age, religion, and physical abilities. Their model is grounded in the feminist political analysis that men's violence against women is rooted in patriarchy and male supremacy. In-depth, eye-opening reading.   nomas.org

NATIONAL WOMEN'S HISTORY MUSEUM is dedicated to uncovering, sharing, and celebrating women's diverse contributions to society. This digital-first museum fills in major omissions of women in history books and K–12 education with scholarly content, resources, and programming for educators and learners of all ages. Two examples: "Where are the Women? A Report on the Status of Women in US Social Studies Standards," and their latest campaign "*she* is not a footnote*" to address the underrepresentation of women in history.   womenshistory.org

Equality • Partnership • Women

RIANE EISLER pioneered the expansion of human rights theory to include the majority of humanity: women and children. Her best-selling book, *The Chalice and the Blade*, in its 57th US printing, revealed the long-ignored role, presence, and contribution of women in the archaeological record, and a new partnership model to replace a millennia of domination. See Center for Partnership Systems and visit her site for more.

rianeeisler.com

SUPPRESSED HISTORIES ARCHIVES was founded by Max Dashu to research and document women's history on a global scale, to find societies where women were free, and to understand how systems of domination establish and perpetuate themselves. She has built a vast collection of images, visual presentations, articles, photo essays, books, and videos to identify cultural heritages that have been hidden. A treasure of information. Free and fee-based programs. suppressedhistories.net

THE REPRESENTATION PROJECT (TRP) produced the groundbreaking film *Miss Representation* igniting a national conversation about sexism in media. Other films challenge the stereotype of masculinity, and address domestic and systemic inequity. TRP utilizes film and media to inspire individuals and communities to challenge limiting gender stereotypes and build a more equitable future for everyone. therepproject.org

Resources

Healthy Mind, Body, Spirit

Many healing resources have been around for centuries: Acupressure, acupuncture, energy medicine, meditation, qigong, reiki, tai chi, and yoga, just to name a few. Often called "alternative," to long-time practitioners they are considered traditional and may complement conventional medicine. Some are included in this section.

ACTION FOR HAPPINESS (England and Wales) helps people create a happier world by providing resources to make happiness and kindness a priority. Check the *Calendar* tab for daily happiness tips and the *Take action* tab for free online coaching, inspiring talks, a *Happiness Habits* course, and more!   actionforhappiness.org

ACUPRESSURE.COM was founded by Michael Reed Gach, Ph.D. to share the benefits of this ancient healing system that uses finger pressure to release blocked energy in the body to heal, balance the emotions, clear the mind, and enhance the spirit for both preventative care and vibrant health. Free videos and articles. Certified training is available. (Also see Further Reading.)   acupressure.com

CDC (CENTERS FOR DISEASE CONTROL AND PREVENTION) is a US science-based, data-driven service organization that protects the public's health. A broad range of *Health Topics* include diseases and conditions, travelers health, and emergency preparedness.   cdc.gov

GREATER GOOD SCIENCE CENTER studies the psychology, sociology, and neuroscience of well-being and teaches skills that foster a thriving, resilient, and compassionate society. Their free online magazine *Greater Good* turns scientific research into stories, tips, and tools for a happy and more meaningful life. Visit *In Action* and *In Education* sites for more!   ggsc.berkeley.edu

HEARTMATH INSTITUTE (HMI) helps people bring their physical, mental, and emotional systems into balanced alignment with their heart's intuitive guidance. Through heart-brain connection research, HMI has developed tools and techniques to enable people everywhere to break through to greater levels of personal balance, creativity, intuitive insight, and fulfillment. Blog articles, videos, tools, and free courses are available.   heartmath.org

Holistic medicine treats the whole person—mind, body, spirit. There are many forms available. Always consult with your healthcare professional to avoid any conflicts and to support existing treatment.

Resources

LOUISE HAY was a pioneer in the modern self-help movement, influencing millions with her positive philosophy and healing techniques. Her popular published reference guides detail the mental/emotional causes of physical ailments, and provide positive thought patterns to reverse illness and create more wellness in our bodies, minds, and spirits. *Wisdom from Louise* and *Affirmations* tabs have immediately useful thoughts.　louisehay.com

MENTAL HEALTH AMERICA is dedicated to the promotion of mental health, well-being, and illness prevention. They work to increase nationwide awareness and understanding through public education, tools, and research. Lots of *Help* and *Information* resources.　mhanational.org

MINDFUL is dedicated to sharing the gifts of mindfulness through content, training, courses, and events—helping people enjoy better health, foster more caring relationships, and cultivate a more compassionate society. Learn how to meditate and reap the benefits of adding mindful practices to your daily life.　mindful.org

NETWORKTHERAPY.COM is an online destination for mental health consumers seeking in-person or telehealth therapy services in the US and Canada. Offers a searchable provider directory as well as articles and links to mental health information, news, support groups, and related resources. Lots of info here!　networktherapy.com

YOQI (yo-chee) is a portal created by Marisa Cranfill. Her YOQI energy routines integrate awareness-based movement and self-healing techniques from two of the most powerful and time tested mind-body-spirit practices today: yoga and qigong. Classes, workshops, free videos and more. yoqi.com

Legal

Legal assistance organizations exist in every US state. Call a local attorney or try an Internet search for legal help in your state (or country). Here are 2 examples in the US.

LEGAL SERVICES CORPORATION (LSC) is a non-profit established by Congress that funds independent organizations around the country to provide civil legal services to low income Americans. Use their *Get Legal Help* button to find an LSC funded legal aid office near you. 202-295-1500 lsc.gov

WOMENSLAW provides plain-language legal information in Spanish and English through their website and *Email Hotline* to anyone, regardless of gender, who reaches out with legal questions or concerns regarding domestic violence, sexual violence, or any other topics they cover. Site includes *Legal Information* by State, *Preparing for Court, About Abuse, Safety Planning*, and *Places that Help*. womenslaw.org

Resources

Parents & Caregivers

CHILD WELFARE INFORMATION GATEWAY connects professionals and concerned citizens to resources on the child welfare continuum that support positive outcomes for all children, youth and families.
800-394-3366 Limited hours.　　　　childwelfare.gov

ELDERCARE LOCATOR connects older Americans and their families with local support resources. Call or search their site for more. (See full listing under FIND.)
800-677-1116 Limited hours.　　　　eldercare.acl.gov

END CORPORAL PUNISHMENT has a vision for a world where children grow up free from violence. Corporal punishment is the most common form of violence against children worldwide. Learn why this initiative is so important, explore their *Resources* for positive parenting, and *About Us* to get involved. (For more insight, see Way #16 Spare the rod.)　　　endcorporalpunishment.org

HEALTHYCHILDREN.ORG is a parenting website from the American Academy of Pediatrics and is backed by 67,000 pediatricians committed to the attainment of optimal physical, mental, and social health and well-being for all infants, children, adolescents, and young adults.

Whether you're looking for general information related to child health or more specific guidance on parenting issues, there's lots to explore here. healthychildren.org

NATIONAL PTA (PARENT TEACHER ASSOCIATION) is a voice for children, families, communities, and public education. (See full listing under Volunteer.)
800-307-4782 (800-307-4PTA) pta.org

PARENTING.ORG, a service of Boys Town, offers a series of guides and tools on a variety of popular parenting topics. The Boys Town National Hotline is also available 24/7 for anyone with a question.
800-448-3000 parenting.org

STOPBULLYING.GOV is an exceptional resource on what bullying is, who is at risk, how you can prevent it, and how to respond. Check it out! (Full listing under Peace-Building.) stopbullying.gov

Peace is more than the absence of violence. Peace is the **presence** of harmony, prosperity, equality, and kindness.

Resources

Peace-Building

KIDS FOR PEACE is building a worldwide community of kind, compassionate and empowered young people. (See full listing under Youth.) kidsforpeaceglobal.org

KINDSPRING is an online community of people who practice small acts of kindness, share stories, and cheer each other on! 100% volunteer-run and totally non-commercial. The *Ideas* tab has lots of inspiration by theme! You can even include your good deeds by clicking the *Count Me* button. Also see their *Smile Cards* campaign! kindspring.org

MY AFFIRMATION PROJECT is a public art project created by artist Nicole Leth to integrate compassion into the world in anonymous, free, and unexpected ways. Think billboards with positive statements, postcards sent anonymously, and more. myaffirmationproject.com

NATIONAL CRIME PREVENTION COUNCIL is home to McGruff the Crime Dog® and helps Americans Take A Bite Out Of Crime® through demonstration programs in schools and neighborhoods, training and support for local crime prevention efforts, and easy to use crime prevention tips and resources. ncpc.org

Peace-Building

NEIGHBORHOOD DAY is all about celebrating neighbors on National Neighborhood Day in September. But why wait? Connecting neighbors builds more satisfying, self-sufficient and effective communities that strengthen our nation as a whole. Check the *Ideas for Gatherings* page and their planning guide and templates to make connecting a whole lot easier!   neighborhoodday.org

PATHWAYS TO PEACE works locally and globally, inter-generationally and multi-culturally to support peace building, peace builders, and collaborate with other organizations to advance a culture of peace. Also learn how you can get involved in the *International Day of Peace* and the *Peace Wave!*   pathwaystopeace.org

PEACE ALLIANCE educates, advocates, and mobilizes for peace. Support their campaign for a US Department of Peacebuilding. Read their "BluePrint for Peace" for proactive, healing-focused approaches to bring peace to our communities, schools, justice systems, international relations, and personal relationships.   peacealliance.org

RANDOM ACTS OF KINDNESS FOUNDATION is dedicated to making kindness the norm by inspiring and facilitating kindness through their free resources focusing on schools, workplaces, and home/communities. Loads of ideas and activities—all to make the world a better place one act of kindness at a time.   randomactsofkindness.org

Resources

STOPBULLYING.GOV is an exceptional resource for information from various government agencies on what bullying is, who is at risk, how you can prevent it, and how to respond. You'll find "How to Talk about Bullying" under *Resources*, and important tips for "Bystanders to Bullying" under *Prevention*. If you are concerned at all and want to know more, visit this site! stopbullying.gov

Positive News & Inspiring Video

Tired of the mainstream flow of negative news? Add one or more of these sites to balance your intake or make it your new go-to news source. Sign up for their newsletter!

DAILYGOOD aims to shine a light on positive and uplifting news from around the world to change the nature of our conversations and spread a few smiles along the way. dailygood.org

GOOD GOOD GOOD reports on positive news with a focus on "real good news" over "feel good news." They highlight "the helpers" working to create solutions to the world's problems, big or small. goodgoodgood.co

GOOD NEWS NETWORK is a clearinghouse for positive news stories from around the globe. Also check their *Morning Jolt* email newsletter. goodnewsnetwork.org

Positive News & Inspiring Video

KARMATUBE is dedicated to bringing inspirational stories to light using video and the Internet to multiply acts of kindness, beauty, and generosity.   karmatube.org

OPTIMIST DAILY offers a daily dose of optimism through good news from around the world to encourage people to start each day with a positive, solution-oriented mindset.
optimistdaily.com

POSITIVE NEWS (United Kingdom) reports socially relevant and uplifting stories of progress showing how people are changing the world for the better.   positive.news

SQUIRREL NEWS (Berlin, Germany) offers a counterbalance and respite from the negativity of mainstream media, and the clickbait, doomsday and profit-driven journalism that often comes with it. Why a squirrel? They are so selective in their picks!   squirrel-news.net

TED spreads ideas that spark conversation, deepen understanding, and drive meaningful change. There are TED Talks, TEDx events, climate-focused content from TED Countdown, TEDNext, and more from science and business to education, arts, and global issues. Short videos are available to the world for free.   ted.com

Good things are happening all the time!

Resources

Volunteer

There are lots of ways to give to your community or a cause you believe in. Find an outlet that fits your schedule and aligns with your passion and interests. You might even learn a new skill and make friends! You could be a phone call away from your next adventure. Any resource in this book likely has opportunities to volunteer in some capacity. Here are 11 more.

IDEALIST is on a mission to bridge the gap between intention and action for social good by connecting individuals, nonprofits, and mission-driven organizations. From jobs and internships, to volunteer opportunities and collective action, Idealist is a global community of changemakers committed to making a difference.   idealist.org

MENTOR offers trained volunteers to help the more than 1 in 3 young people who lack or simply want the support of more caring adults in their life. A mentoring relationship can foster positive development by showing young people that there is someone who cares about them, assures them they are not alone in dealing with day-to-day challenges, and makes them feel like they matter. Use their search tool to find or become a mentor.
617-303-4600   mentoring.org

NATIONAL CASA/GAL ASSOCIATION FOR CHILDREN is a network of trained volunteers who advocate for the best interests of children and youth who have experienced abuse or neglect. Volunteers work with legal and child welfare professionals, educators, service providers, and the foster care system to ensure that judges have the information they need to make the most well-informed decisions for each child. Search for a local program and learn how you can speak up for a child.
800-628-3233 nationalcasagal.org

NATIONAL LITERACY DIRECTORY is a free online directory funded by Dollar General Literacy Foundation that lists organizations providing federal-, state-, and public-funded education programs for adults and families. Potential students and literacy volunteers can call the toll-free number or search their website to locate nearby educational programs and services.
877-389-6874 nld.org

NATIONAL PTA (PARENT TEACHER ASSOCIATION) prides itself as a powerful voice for all children, a relevant resource for families and communities, and a strong advocate for public education. Contact National PTA for more and to locate a local unit. Also, PTA websites are not the same, so check out other state sites for ideas and resources to benefit our kids!
800-307-4782 (800-307-4PTA) pta.org

Resources

UNITED NATIONS (UN) is a global organization with main offices in New York, Geneva, Nairobi, Vienna, and the Hague. The UN is the place where all the world's nations can gather together, discuss common problems, and find shared solutions that benefit all of humanity. Learn more through the *Our Work* tab, and check out the *Get Involved* section for jobs and volunteer opportunities. Scroll to the bottom of every UN page for a list of *Resources/Services, Issues/Campaigns,* and more. Four UN programs follow. See all programs at... un.org

UNITED NATIONS ASSOCIATION OF THE USA has over 20,000 members and more than 200 chapters across the US dedicated to educating, inspiring, and mobilizing support for the principles and vital work of the UN and its agencies. Visit their site, find or start a local chapter, and continue this peacekeeping work.

unausa.org

UNICEF (UNITED NATIONS CHILDREN'S FUND) works in over 190 countries and territories to save children's lives, defend their rights, and help them fulfill their potential from early childhood through adolescence. UNICEF also provides full text and child friendly versions of the *Convention on the Rights of the Child*, an historic commitment by world leaders. Check the *Take Action* tab for more. unicef.org

UN OFFICE OF THE HIGH COMMISSIONER FOR HUMAN RIGHTS (Geneva) is the leading UN entity on human rights. The Office represents the world's commitment to the promotion and protection of the full range of human rights and freedoms set out in the *Universal Declaration of Human Rights* (see Further Reading). Learn about *Human Rights, Topics* they support, how to *Get Involved*, and more.   ohchr.org

UN WOMEN is dedicated to gender equality and the empowerment of women, and was established to accelerate progress on meeting the needs of women and girls worldwide. Check out their active campaigns to see how you can *Get Involved*, and the *Commission on the Status of Women* to learn about their ongoing global policy-making work.   unwomen.org

It may seem a little intimidating to consider getting involved with an organization like the United Nations, but every person working, consulting with, or volunteering for them may have once held some doubt. Imagine the difference you could make!

Resources

WORLD WILDLIFE FUND works with people across the globe to develop and deliver innovative solutions that protect communities, wildlife, and wild places. Check their *Get Involved* tab to *Take Action,* access *Educational Resources*, *Send a (wildlife) Ecard* to friends and family, and more. worldwildlife.org

Youth *Action*

4-H (Head, Heart, Hands, and Health) programs empower young people of all beliefs and backgrounds to unlock their potential through hands-on projects in areas like health, science, agriculture, and civic engagement. Adult mentors provide leadership skills in a positive environment to encourage kids and teens to make great things happen for themselves, their families, and their communities. Use the search tool to find a club near you.   4-h.org

DO SOMETHING is a youth-centered activism and service hub committed to educating and equipping young people for social change around equity and justice, climate and sustainability, and safety and well-being. Members in every US area code and 189 countries are taking action to improve their communities by working on causes they care about. Lots of ideas!   dosomething.org

KIDS FOR PEACE is building a worldwide community of kind, compassionate, and empowered young people. Programs include *The Peace Pledge Program* (chapter-based where kids discuss peace and take action to create a better world) and *The Great Kindness Challenge* (an annual week-long event to create a culture of kindness on school campuses). Visit their site for more information, to start a chapter, or to print their *Peace Pledge* for your home or workplace. kidsforpeaceglobal.org

Youth *Info*

LOVE IS RESPECT (a project of the National Domestic Violence Hotline) offers 24/7 information, support, and advocacy to young people ages 13 to 26 who have questions or concerns about their romantic relationships. Concerned friends, family members, and service providers can get the same support via phone, text, and chat.
866-331-9474   loveisrespect.org

THE JED FOUNDATION (JED) builds resiliency and life skills, promotes social connection, and encourages help-seeking and -giving behaviors in our nation's teens and young adults by partnering with high schools and colleges to strengthen their mental health and well-being programs. For the giver and the receiver, the *Resource Center* has lots of supportive content.   jedfoundation.org

Resources

YOUR LIFE YOUR VOICE, a service of BoysTown, is a place for teens, pre-teens, and young adults to get age appropriate answers on everyday challenges such as anxiety, friendship, bullying, and dating; as well as kindness, journaling, and happiness. Click on a topic for lots of articles, tips, and tools. Options to contact a counselor via text, email, or the Boys Town National Hotline.
800-448-3000   yourlifeyourvoice.org

Youth *Programs*

BOYS & GIRLS CLUBS OF AMERICA provide caring mentors, a safe place, and innovative, quality programs designed to empower all youth to excel in school and lead healthy, productive lives. Check their *Programs*, *Get Involved*, and *Find a Club* sections for more.   bgca.org

MENTOR, at its core, aims to guarantee young people that there is someone who cares about them, assures them they are not alone in dealing with day-to-day challenges, and makes them feel like they matter. (See full listing under Volunteer.)
617-303-4600   mentoring.org

NATIONAL CASA/GAL ASSOCIATION FOR CHILDREN is a network of trained volunteers that represent the best interests of abused and neglected children in the courtroom and other settings. (See full listing under Volunteer.)

800-628-3233   nationalcasagal.org

They are all daisies

and each one is unique,

just like *you*.

What's that little number next to each organization listed under Phone Numbers and Websites?

It's the page number where you'll find their listing or more info about them! =)

Phone Numbers

National Emergency Number 175   911

Hotlines & Helplines

Suicide & Crisis Lifeline 175   988
Boys Town National Hotline 176   800-448-3000
Childhelp Nat'l Child Abuse Hotline 176   800-422-4453
Love is Respect 203   866-331-9474
National Domestic Violence Hotline 176   800-799-7233
National Human Trafficking Hotline 177   888-373-7888

Information / FIND

CDC-INFO 177   800-232-4636
Eldercare Locator 178   800-677-1116
Legal Services Corporation 191   202-295-1500
USA.gov 179   844-872-4681
US Dept. of Health & Human Services 179   877-696-6775

Other Listed Phone Numbers

Child Welfare Information Gateway 196   800-394-3366
Great Courses Plus, The 182   800-832-2412
Mentor 198   617-303-4600
Nat'l CASA/GAL Assoc. for Children 199   800-628-3233

Websites

National Literacy Directory [199]   877-389-6874
National Parent Teacher Association [199]   800-307-4782
Parenting.org (via Boys Town) [193]   800-448-3000
Poison Control [243]   800-222-1222
US Capitol Switchboard [108]   202-224-3121
Your Life Your Voice (via Boys Town) [204] 800-448-3000

Websites

4-H [202]   4-h.org
911 National Emergency Number Assoc. [175]   nena.org
988 Suicide & Crisis Lifeline [175]   988lifeline.org
Action for Happiness [188]   actionforhappiness.org
Acupressure.com [188]   acupressure.com
Adult Survivors of Child Abuse [183]   ascasupport.org
Americans for the Arts [181]   americansforthearts.org
Blue Knot [183]   blueknot.org.au
Boys & Girls Clubs of America [204]   bgca.org
Boys Town National Hotline [176]   boystown.org/hotline
Canadian Women's Foundation [184]   canadianwomen.org
CDC-INFO [177]   cdc.gov/cdc-info
Center for Partnership Systems [185]   centerforpartnership.org
Centers for Disease Control & Prevention [188]   cdc.gov
Childhelp National Child Abuse Hotline [176]   childhelphotline.org

Websites

Child Helpline Int'l 178	childhelplineinternational.org
Child Welfare Information Gateway 192	childwelfare.gov
Coursera 182	coursera.org
Daily Good 196	dailygood.org
Domestic Shelters 184	domesticshelters.org
Do Something 202	dosomething.org
Eldercare Locator 178	eldercare.acl.gov
End Corporal Punishment 192	endcorporalpunishment.org
Equal Rights Amendment 185	equalrightsamendment.org
Equimundo: Center for Masculinities and Social Justice 186	equimundo.org
Good Good Good 196	goodgoodgood.co
Good News Network 196	goodnewsnetwork.org
Great Courses Plus, The 182	thegreatcoursesplus.com
Greater Good Science Center 189	ggsc.berkeley.edu
Healthy Children 192	healthychildren.org
HeartMath Institute 189	heartmath.org
Help for Adult Victims of Child Abuse 184	havoca.org
Idealist 198	idealist.org
Inspired 101 142	inspired101.com
Jed Foundation, The 203	jedfoundation.org
KarmaTube 197	karmatube.org
Kids for Peace 203	kidsforpeaceglobal.org
KindSpring 194	kindspring.org
Legal Services Corporation 191	lsc.gov

Websites

Louise Hay [190] louisehay.com
Love is Respect [203] loveisrespect.org
Mental Health America [190] mhanational.org
Mentor [198] mentoring.org
Mindful [190] mindful.org
My Affirmation Project [194] myaffirmationproject.com
Nat'l Assembly of State Arts Agencies [181] nasaa-arts.org
National CASA/GAL Association for Children [199]
nationalcasagal.org
National Crime Prevention Council [194] ncpc.org
National Domestic Violence Hotline [176] thehotline.org
National Endowment for the Arts [181] arts.gov
National Human Trafficking Hotline [177]
humantraffickinghotline.org
National Literacy Directory [199] nld.org
Nat'l Organization for Men against Sexism [186] nomas.org
National Parent Teacher Association [199] pta.org
Nat'l Women's History Museum [186] womenshistory.org
Neighborhood Day [195] neighborhoodday.org
NetworkTherapy [190] networktherapy.com
Office for Victims of Crime [179] ovc.ojp.gov
OpenLearn [182] openlearn.com
Optimist Daily, The [197] optimistdaily.com
Parenting.org [193] parenting.org
Pathways To Peace [195] pathwaystopeace.org

Websites

Peace Alliance [195]	peacealliance.org
Positive News [197]	positive.news
Random Acts of Kindness [195]	randomactsofkindness.org
Representation Project, The [187]	therepproject.org
Riane Eisler [187]	rianeeisler.com
Squirrel News [197]	squirrel-news.net
StopBullying.gov [196]	stopbullying.gov
Suppressed Histories Archives [187]	suppressedhistories.net
Survivors [184]	survivors.org
TED [197]	ted.com
Udemy [182]	udemy.com
United Nations [200]	un.org
United Nations Association of the USA [200]	unausa.org
United Nations Children's Fund [200]	unicef.org
UN Office of the High Commissioner for Human Rights [201]	ohchr.org
UN Women [201]	unwomen.org
USA.gov [179]	usa.gov
US Department of Health & Human Services [179]	hhs.gov
Warmline Directory [180]	warmline.org
WomensLaw.org [191]	womenslaw.org
World Wildlife Fund [202]	worldwildlife.org
YOQI [191]	yoqi.com
Your Life Your Voice [204]	yourlifeyourvoice.org

The Inspiration

The first edition of this book was based on my list of "101 Things You Can Do To Prevent Child Abuse" reflecting my experience and insights as a survivor, child advocate, and over 30 years in human behavior and potential.

The Back Story

As a victim I learned to be quiet, observant, and careful. I watched how people interacted. That curiosity turned into a passion for understanding. Why do we do the things we do? I became fascinated with the study of **handwriting** and the insight it provides into character and personality. As a very shy person, this was the perfect tool to learn about others without having to talk to them. Oddly enough, my confidence in this skill is what helped me find my voice.

Later, countless analyses proved that we may share similar traits like generosity, sensitivity, and imagination, but our experience and perception will determine how we direct that energy. I also learned that we all have stuff—fears not reconciled, a reality we are not ready to face, or difficulties we are working through—yet, we are amazing creatures still; not only for what we accomplish or dream of doing, but simply because we are here.

The Inspiration

Years later, that insight had to be turned inward. A flood of memories had to be acknowledged and reconciled before I could move forward. My **healing** became a priority. I stopped and started plenty of times but, when I persevered and faced the monsters on my path, my recovery became truly profound. The fear, anger, and hurt dissolved. I understood, and with that came compassion and a resolve to do something to stop the cycle of abuse—it became a beacon.

When a friend suggested a program that was dedicated to providing a **voice** for abused children in court, I was eager to apply my experience and passion toward such a positive goal. I threw myself into this work and was honored by the governor's office for my dedication.

Yet, to **my surprise** it was the child protection system that presented the greatest challenge. Somehow I expected everyone involved to *get it,* to understand the dynamic of abuse, but not everyone did. Some had wounds to heal while others lacked the necessary training, and many organizations within the network of responders were understaffed and overwhelmed. Although important and necessary services were being provided, this system couldn't do it all.

Then there was a meeting with the director of a nonprofit for child abuse prevention. I wanted to share some ideas. He focused more on their current drive to collect stuffed animals for the previous year's victims. It was more of an awareness campaign, he said. A worthy

endeavor for sure but all I could think was:
There is so much more we can do!

The List

Like what? I asked myself on the drive home. I thought about what survivors may not have experienced; the good things like healthy interaction, loving support, encouragement for their growing interests and skills, and safety in their own homes. I imagined a world where children were not abused. In that space, *The List* came tumbling out—all of the original 101 Things. I pulled over to write them down as quickly as they came. It stopped at about 93. I drove the rest of the way home, added a few more, and the list of "101 Things You Can Do to Prevent Child Abuse" was born.

That was my focus then. But even then I knew it was more than preventing child abuse. It was an empowering and positive **call to action**.

Q & A with Debbie

Why is this so important to you?

I am a survivor of child abuse. I know what it's like to feel unloved, invisible, and worthless. If we don't reconcile those feelings and recognize them as not ours but our offenders, then they win over and over again as we allow their beliefs to direct our actions. We have to remember our value, regardless of how we have been treated. Each of us has great gifts to share. It is so wildly unfair to be silenced because of the actions of others.

All things considered, how can you be so positive?

Because I've been to the dark side. This book is a testament to my survival. I shouldn't be here, and I'm not the only one whose faced horrendously dark times. But at some point, we have to separate from the harm inflicted on us and realize it was actually not about us at all. We were just there. We are not here to suffer. It helps to remember who we are, before all the challenges and tragedies of this life, because that is our authentic nature. It also helps to view our experience as integral to our lives in some way.

In my survival and in my recovery, I was drawn to alternative healing such as altered states, meditation, handwriting analysis, acupressure, energy medicine, and animal symbology. Each broadened—and brightened—

my understanding of self and spirit, making me realize how truly amazing we are, yet we are often taught and encouraged to believe otherwise. That's the lie. I think of it this way: Love is our core and our source, and light is our expression. It's up to us to find the best ways to express that love. In so doing we light the way for others. It really is a happy thought. And the more positive thoughts we experience, well… It's not rocket science. It's simple math and it's all kind of magical.

This is the 2nd edition. Why publish a revision?

Because the information, ideas, and resources are still relevant. While the 1st edition—published 11 years ago but written 23 years ago—focused on child abuse, the intention was and still is to share the power of reflection, healing, and especially positive action.

With so much violence and negativity, then and now, I find that most people still don't know what to do. Any conversation tends to focus on the size, scope, details, and horror. People are quickly overwhelmed until they're numbed by it. We analyze every aspect of what's wrong and spend little time and energy on solutions. It should be the reverse. And reminders can keep us on track.

How can we solve a problem if we don't focus on it?

Every problem comes with a solution. The key is, once we identify what we don't want (the problem), then all our focus needs to go on creating what we do want, because that's how we'll get there. We can leave the important research on the problem and its causes to data analysts, leaving more room for the rest of us to to put the solutions in motion, thereby addressing the problem while keeping it in perspective.

Why not just go with a simple List?

Life is not a sound bite or an emoji. While a list is nice for easy referral, I want the reader to grasp the fullness of my intent to spark ideas that are unique to them and their situation. Besides, I always like to know *the why* of one's creation, so I have presented each of the *Ways* with a paragraph of insight and perspective to encourage a sense of self awareness, acceptance, and forward movement.

Why did you change the title of the list?

With the first edition, I truly believed the phrase *child abuse* had to be stated to make it easier to talk about. But the reality is people don't want to talk about it, even in a positive and inspiring solutions-based context. That edition read like a list of happy thoughts, and people are just not used to thinking that way, much less in relation to an issue that thrives in secrecy. So I changed the title to reflect the intention which has always been to wow our world with love and kindness. In the process—if we're diligent—we will create an environment where things like violence, abuse, and disrespect cannot thrive.

Q & A with Debbie

Tell us about the other big changes.

I agonized over making any changes to the original list because of the magical way it appeared. But I also knew that had I not created the first list of *101 Things* and not trusted my experience, perspective, and process, this list of *101 Ways* wouldn't exist.

Some of the original *Things* are retitled and rearranged. Also, there were five *nevers* that I felt needed to be clearly stated at the time: Never hit your child. Never hit any person. Never belittle a child. Never use a child for sexual gratification. Never torture a child. In the new edition, all *101 Ways* are positive actions reflecting desired outcomes. Those five are still there, but are rephrased, merged, or under a new heading.

What surprised you the most about this new edition?

I thought it would be easy and quick: fix some typos, change the *nevers*, update the design, and add some resources, but I also wanted to add some concepts that were especially helpful to me, like *#5. Honor the spirit in others, #36. Remember your magnificence,* and *#84. Release the (k)nots.* So it took longer than I expected. Plus there's so much good stuff out there! At some point, I had to stop revising, stop exploring new resources, and publish.

What is the most important Way?

On any day I might give you a different answer. But if I could only name one, it would be *#101. Love more.* We need a more complete understanding of love, how we use the word and our experience of it. With that awareness, our expression of love, our choosing loving actions and words becomes easier, more authentic, and more wide reaching. It's what we all want. When all is said and done, we need to love a whole lot more.

Acknowledgments

This edition was created in a spiritual cocoon, starting in earnest during the isolating COVID years. Eventually the why of the cocoon became clear: this book had to remain in my voice from my experience and perspective.

I think of women who under threat of harm, imprisonment, ridicule, and banishment told their stories, shared their perspectives, and documented their ideas and their research. They spoke about the influence, importance, and accomplishments of women; many reinterpreting the symbols, artifacts, and feminine presence in the archaeological record dating back tens of thousands of years countering the notion that women had no real significance in that story. Sheesh! I thank those writers for lighting the way with their courage, insight, and example. Then I think of the countless number who were silenced; I feel compelled to write in their honor. I might have remained silent if not for Anne Selten whose guidance, wisdom, and Spirit are with me to this day.

Other rays of light made it into the cocoon, like Anne Sophie Hug with her input on rephrasing the *nevers*, Larry Yamamoto—a fan since my handwriting analysis column days in Hawaii, and Paula Shelton, Meg Jansen, and

Acknowledgments

Brecia Kralovic-Logan whose comments and anecdotes in response to my newsletters—which continued from the cocoon—reflected exactly what I wanted my writing to be. And to Karen Dodson, who always asked about the book and always showed interest in its progress. For our coffee chats and to you I am forever grateful.

And finally to the people I contacted within the organizations in the resources section. Many were so positive and optimistic about being listed. Their passion and enthusiasm matched my intention for this project—and reminded me of the light outside of the cocoon.

I thank you all.

Bibliography

This list includes works cited as well as other media mentioned.

Adult Survivors of Child Abuse (ASCA). "Survivor to Thriver Manual," accessed August 29, 2024. https://ascasupport.org/materials/

Canadian Women's Foundation. "Violence at Home #SignalForHelp". September 27, 2020. YouTube video, 1:00, https://www.youtube.com/watch?v=AFLZEQFIm7k

Center for Partnership Systems."Caring and Connected Parenting: A Guide to Raising Connected Children," accessed August 29, 2024. https://centerforpartnership.org/programs/caring_and_connected_parenting_guide/

Cohen, Randy. "10 Reasons to Support the Arts in 2024," accessed June 9, 2025. https://www.americansforthearts.org/by-topic/advancing-arts-locally/top-10-reasons-to-support-the-arts

End Corporal Punishment. "Progress," accessed April 8, 2025. https://endcorporalpunishment.org/countdown/

——— "Reforming national laws to prohibit corporal punishment," accessed May 20, 2024. https://endcorporalpunishment.org/reforming-national-laws/

——— "Corporal punishment of children in the USA," updated August 2024. https://www.endcorporalpunishment.org/wp-content/uploads/country-reports/USA.pdf.

Equimundo: Center for Masculinities and Social Justice. "State of American Men 2025." https://www.equimundo.org/resources/state-of-american-men-2025/

——— "State of the World's Fathers 2023: Centering Care in a World in Crisis." https://www.equimundo.org/resources/state-of-the-worlds-fathers-2023/

Jenae, Debbie. *Your Light, Your Life! 10 Best Pep Talks Ever.* Inspired 101, 2021.

Bibliography

Kids For Peace Global. "Peace Pledge," accessed March 21, 2024. https://kidsforpeaceglobal.org//wp-content/uploads/2017/04/Peace-Pledge-Postcard.jpg

National Women's History Museum. "Where are the Women? A Report on the Status of Women in the United States Social Studies Standards," 2017. https://www.womenshistory.org/social-studies-standards

Nonprofits Source. "Volunteering Statistics And Trends For Nonprofits," accessed October 23, 2023. https://nonprofitssource.com/online-giving-statistics/volunteering-statistics/

Representation Project, The. "Miss Representation," (documentary/movie), 2011. https://therepproject.org/films/

Ritchie, Hannah. "How many species are there?" Our World In Data, November 30, 2022. https://ourworldindata.org/how-many-species-are-there

Solan, Matthew. "Ease anxiety and stress: Take a (belly) breather," Harvard Health Blog, May 10, 2022. https://www.health.harvard.edu/blog/ease-anxiety-and-stress-take-a-belly-breather-2019042616521

Stibich, Mark. "10 Big Benefits of Smiling," Very Well Mind, updated February 17, 2023. https://www.verywellmind.com/top-reasons-to-smile-every-day-2223755

United Nations. UN Committee on the Rights of the Child (CRC), General comment No. 8 (2006): The Right of the Child to Protection from Corporal Punishment and Other Cruel or Degrading Forms of Punishment (III Definitions, Para. 11), CRC/C/GC/8, 2 March 2007, accessed July 14, 2025. https://www.refworld.org/legal/general/crc/2007/en/41020

Further Reading

The first two of these UN documents are mentioned elsewhere in the text, but I've listed them here because they are worth a read. My comments are in parentheses.

United Nations Documents

United Nations. *United Nations Convention on the Rights of the Child* (CRC) was adopted in 1989 by UN General Assembly resolution 44/25. https://www.unicef.org/child-rights-convention. (196 countries have consented to the CRC. The United States of America is the only country that has not ratified this human rights treaty.)

United Nations. *Universal Declaration of Human Rights* was adopted in 1948 by the UN General Assembly resolution 217A. https://www.ohchr.org/en/universal-declaration-of-human-rights. (The Declaration was created in response to the atrocities of the second world war. It guarantees the rights of every individual everywhere.)

United Nations Children's Fund. *The State of the World's Children* is UNICEF's flagship report—the most comprehensive analysis of global trends affecting children. View the latest here: https://www.unicef.org/reports/state-of-worlds-children

Select Books & Media

These are some of the books that were helpful to me in my journey. Newer editions may be available. My comments are in parentheses.

Andrews, Ted. *Animal-Speak: The Spiritual & Magical Powers of Creatures Great & Small.* Llewellyn Publications, 1993. (An amazing look at what the animal world can teach us.)

Further Reading

Bass, Ellen and Laura Davis. *The Courage to Heal: A Guide for Women Survivors of Child Sexual Abuse.* Harper & Row Publishers, Inc., 1988. (A pioneering work offering validation, hope, and healing for survivors and those who care about them.)

Bunker, M. N. *Handwriting Analysis: The Science of Determining Personality by Graphoanalysis.* Nelson-Hall Co., Publishers, 1969. (One of the first books I read about handwriting analysis. I've been hooked ever since!)

Carter, Jimmy. *A Call to Action: Women, Religion, Violence, and Power.* Simon & Schuster, 2014. (Explores the world's discrimination and violence against women and girls.)

Chopra, Deepak *Ageless Body, Timeless Mind: The Quantum Alternative to Growing Old.* Harmony Books, 1993. (How our mind affects our whole body health.)

Eisler, Riane. *The Chalice and the Blade: Our history, our future.* HarperCollins Publishers, Inc., 1988. (Groundbreaking, eye-opening work on the ancient evidence of the story, presence, and contribution of women.)

Eisler, Riane and Douglas P. Fry. *Nurturing our Humanity: How Domination and Partnership Shape our Brains, Lives, and Future.* Oxford University Press, 2019.

Gach, Michael Reed. *Acupressure's Potent Points: A Guide to Self-Care for Common Ailments.* Bantam Books, 1990. (An excellent guide to an ancient healing system to release blockages and balance energy through the use of finger pressure.)

Gage, Matilda Joslyn. *Woman, Church, & State. The Original Exposé of Male Collaboration Against the Female Sex.* First published in 1893, now in the public domain. Retrieved December 28, 2024, from www.gutenberg.org/ebooks/45580. (A fascinating and detailed look at women's prominence in the pre-Christian era and how it all changed.)

Gawain, Shakti with Lauren King. *Living in the Light.* Whatever Publishing, 1986; New World Library, 2011. (Thoughtful reminders, exercises, and meditations to remind us to follow our inner guidance.)

Further Reading

Hawn, Goldie with Wendy Holden, *10 Mindful Minutes: Giving Our Children—and Ourselves— the Social and Emotional Skills to Reduce Stress and Anxiety for Healthier, Happier Lives.* Perigree by the Penguin Group, 2012.

Hay, Louise. *You Can Heal Your Life.* Hay House, 1999. (A groundbreaking book on how limiting and negative beliefs are often the cause of illness. Includes a list of ailments with new thoughts and affirmations to improve health and well-being.)

Oswald, Yvonne. *Every Word Has Power: Switch on Your Language and Turn on Your Life.* Atria Books, 2008. (Tips, stories, and exercises for language awareness for positive change.)

Steinem, Gloria. *Revolution from Within: A Book of Self-Esteem.* Little, Brown & Company, 1992. (The importance of valuing the self and the effect that has in society; notably democracy, injustice, politics, education, equality.)

Tippett, Constance. *Goddess Timeline.* A chronological record of archaeological images of women and goddesses dating back to 30,000 BCE. Accessed December 30, 2024. https://goddesstimeline.com. (An important visual timeline and feminine perspective on the presence and influence of women. Videos also available.)

Tolle, Eckhart. *The Power of Now: A Guide to Spiritual Enlightenment.* New World Library, 2004. (All about living in the moment to experience more joy, presence, and connection.)

Illustrations

The hand drawn daisies springing up throughout this book were created for this edition by this author. Why daisies? Because they seem like such happy flowers! (See more *why* inside front cover.) The smiling sun is also my creation. *Illustrations* listed in this section are photographs unless noted. My comments appear in parentheses.

In order of appearance

Note: The Shasta Daisy and Globe Earth World images were used to create the **daisy/earth combo** image appearing on the covers and on the 2-page *List* spread.

Kirtlane, **Shasta Daisy**, Pixabay.com, accessed February 27, 2024, https://pixabay.com/photos/shasta-daisy-white-flower-blossom-4347653/

Gerd Altmann, **Globe Earth World**, stock illustration, Pixabay.com, accessed May 1, 2024, https://pixabay.com/illustrations/globe-earth-world-globalization-563239/

Anyaberkut, **Yoga and Meditation** woman on beach, Dreamstime.com, accessed October 18, 2023, https://www.dreamstime.com/yoga-meditation-yoga-meditation-concept-background-silhouette-beach-image114402872

Darius Strazdas, **Wet dog shaking water**, Dreamstime.com, accessed June 4, 2024, https://www.dreamstime.com/wet-dog-shaking-water-off-coat-droplets-visible-background-blue-sea-image118758178

Canadian Women's Foundation, *Signal for Help*, image, April 2020, https://canadianwomen.org/signal-for-help/

Osetrik, **Mare and her foal**, Shutterstock.com, accessed October 20, 2023, https://www.shutterstock.com/image-photo/portrait-mare-her-foal-rye-field-25299756

Illustrations

Alex Pentek, ***Kindred Spirits***, sculpture, 2015. www.alexpentek.com/. Photo by Red Power Media. (Between 1830 and 1850 an estimated 100,000 indigenous people, including the Choctaw, were forced to relocate by the US government. Their journey of hunger, exposure, disease, and death is known as the Trail of Tears. In Ireland, The Great Famine from 1845 to 1852 affected nearly 3 million people. An estimated 1 million people died; 2-3 million emigrated to escape poverty, disease, and starvation.)

paladin13, **Notebook and coffee**, iStock.com, accessed August 21, 2024, https://www.istockphoto.com/photo/notebook-and-coffee-on-wooden-table-gm494826666-77668421

Debbie Jenae, *Water lily*, 2013, personal collection.

Debbie Jenae, *Love Rising*, 2024, personal collection. (Recent photo taken of a small section of a much larger chalk drawing created in 2020 during COVID and maintained since then.)

Debbie Jenae, **Stone steps**, 2023, personal collection.

New Africa, **Man holding envelope** with card, Shutterstock.com, accessed October 20, 2023, https://www.shutterstock.com/image-photo/man-holding-envelope-greeting-card-home-1992311906

Kessa, **Kitten in tree**, Pixabay.com, accessed October 18, 2023, https://pixabay.com/photos/cat-kitten-tree-curious-tabby-1647775/

AzamKamolov, **US Capitol** Washington DC, vector graphic, Pixabay.com, accessed May 1, 2024, https://pixabay.com/vectors/us-capitol-washington-dc-1533368/

Woraphon Banchobdi, **Mother daughter yoga**, Dreamstime.com, accessed October 18, 2023, https://www.dreamstime.com/stock-images-mother-daughter-doing-yoga-top-mountain-image40466334

garten-gg, **Balloons**, Pixabay.com, accessed October 18, 2023, https://pixabay.com/photos/emotions-vacation-vacations-clouds-3459666/

Illustrations

HannamariaH, **Silhouette 10 young women**, iStock.com, accessed August 21, 2024, https://www.istockphoto.com/photo/friendship-gm145995617-603435 1?clarity=false

FatCamera, **Vibrant senior woman in kayak**, iStock.com, accessed April 2, 2024, https://www.istockphoto.com/photo/oregon-coast-kayaking-adventure-gm897329632-247665740

Korn Vitthayanukarun, **Girl teen smiling and reach**, Dreamstime.com, accessed April 1, 2024, https://www.dreamstime.com/girl-teen-smiling-reach-her-hand-help-touch-care-support-be-good-friend-love-concept-image160617886

FatCamera, **Children throwing leaves**, iStock.com, accessed April 2, 2024, https://www.istockphoto.com/photo/throwing-leaves-gm843813482-138078771

Debbie Jenae, *Choose Happy*, billboard, 2024, personal collection. Used with permission from Lamar Advertising Company. (Lamar has been known to use unsold billboard space for positive messages. This one appeared in the Palm Springs area of California.)

Debbie Jenae, *Peace Love Joy*, painted rocks, 2022, personal collection.

Inga-Av, **Man silhouette looking at galaxy**, iStock.com, accessed April 2, 2024, https://www.istockphoto.com/photo/the-man-silhouette-with-camera-and-tripod-stands-on-the-hill-and-looking-at-the-gm1306714918-397217497

Kevin Belstler, **About the Author** photo, 2017.

Debbie Jenae, *Candle to candle*, 2012, personal collection.

Index

A
advocacy 109, 203, 215
advocate 67, 181, 185, 199.
  See volunteer
affirmation 128, 137, 194
animals 72, 101, 158, 219
anonymous 40, 167, 194
appreciate xvi, 36, 50, 59,
  94, 96, 99, 106, 139, 144
arts 73, 180, 194
authentic 7, 48, 67, 79, 140
awareness 13, 56, 111–112,
  122, 150
awareness/denial dynamic xiv

B
balance 26, 48, 70, 92, 126
beacon 106, 114, 216
becoming, adventure of 65
blessing 37, 138
Bonus 13, 71, 127
boundaries 89–90, 122, 157
brain
  and handwriting 54
  healthy play 69

heart connection 189
  learning 102
breath 16, 144
  belly breathing 22
bridge 66, 76, 118
bullying 33, 196, 204
bystander xiv, 33, 196

C
calendar 43, 82, 87
candle 141, 246
capitol switchboard 108
caregiver 28, 165, 178,
  180, 192
celebrate 58, 76, 135, 161
cell phones 81
cherish 17, 34, 66, 82, 96,
  132, 154
child xvii, 8, 23, 27–29,
  31, 33, 46–48, 50, 52,
  99, 103, 154, 166
childhood 101, 150
  UN Convention on the
    Rights of the Child 50
Choctaw Nation 45, 233

Index

communication 53–54, 60, 86, 88, 90, 111, 150, 170
community 10, 27, 41, 53, 57, 73, 106, 109, 112, 131, 157
compassion 38, 130, 158
conflict 28, 119, 161
continuing education 182
control xiii–xv, 9, 16–17, 30, 60, 62, 88, 150, 154
corporal punishment 29, 192
counseling 40, 157, 167
courage 62, 135, 153, 168
courtesy 80, 89, 158
create 23, 56, 60, 68, 82, 86, 91, 103, 124, 127, 130, 141, 143, 154, 161
creativity 39, 48, 69, 73–74, 99, 132, 158
criticism xv, 69, 106, 118, 126, 128
curious 118, 158
  curiosity xvi, 48, 72, 106, 144, 215

D

development 36, 48, 69, 154
discipline 28, 60
dream 79, 101, 140, 150
dynamic xiv, 30, 86, 132, 216

E

e-etiquette
  cell phones 81, 87
  device-free 58, 81
emergency 21, 165, 174–175
empower 39, 133, 157, 183
energy ix, xiii, xvi, 16, 25, 42, 56, 68, 71, 89, 110, 123, 129, 139–140, 144
equality xiii, 110, 132–133, 158, 185

F

family 30, 43, 58, 61, 81–82, 86–87, 154
famine 45, 233
fear ix, xv, 9, 23, 28, 59–60, 78, 90, 111, 161, 215–216
feminine xiii, 132, 185, 225, 231
forgive 123, 150
freedom 48, 50, 201
future 7, 50, 112, 124

G

gift 7, 9, 57, 80, 83, 92, 96, 112, 128, 154, 157

Index

H
habits 23, 26, 68, 79, 90, 120–121, 158, 188
handwriting 54, 215, 219
handwritten 93, 108
heal xiv, xvi, 40, 60, 63, 67, 73, 77, 138, 144, 153
helpline 20, 174–175, 209
history xvi, 56, 77, 187
holistic xiii, 189
honesty 38, 77
hotline 153, 174–179, 191, 193, 203–204, 209
human rights 50, 185, 187, 201, 229
humanity 83, 132, 187, 200

I
imagination xiv, 47–48, 53, 74, 93, 100–101, 132
inner
  calm 26
  dialogue 121
  guidance 170
  knowing 52
innerwhelm xi, 76, 144
innocence 103, 150
inspire ix, 25, 36, 73, 79, 117, 136, 144, 157, 215

integrity 32, 46, 153

J
journal 23, 137, 204
journey 62, 79, 99, 150
joy 56, 90, 103, 111, 114, 123, 126–127, 144, 158

K
kindness xvi, 43, 45, 72, 76, 80, 93, 107, 113, 122, 137, 144, 158
Kindred Spirits 45, 233

L
language 12, 27, 53, 80, 113, 120, 133
legal 109, 157, 191
legislator 108, 157
library 10–11, 47, 109, 166
light 7, 56, 79, 114, 140, 246
love iv, 12, 28–29, 42, 50, 56–57, 59, 70–71, 78–79, 88, 100, 116–117, 126, 138, 144, 150, 154, 161, 220, 223

M
magic 83–84, 144, 220, 222
magnificence xiii, xvii, 56, 161

Index

media xv, 26, 45, 61, 91, 100, 111, 133
mentor 49, 157
mindful xvi, 12–14, 22, 50, 76, 112, 133, 150, 188
miracles 76, 139, 161

N
Namaste 12
nature 7, 71–72, 127, 158
news xiii, xv, 26, 100, 111, 121, 126
nots, the 120, 161

O
opportunity xvi, 27, 29, 37–38, 57, 59, 81, 119, 126, 130, 161

P
pain 28, 52, 56, 68, 116–117, 123, 127
parent 28, 33, 38, 52, 86, 97, 154, 165, 192
partnership 185, 187
patriarchal xiv, 132
peace xv, 28, 106–107, 126, 130, 158, 193
Peace Pledge 106, 203
play 46, 69, 97, 113, 154
police 31, 175, 177

police welfare check 31
political 110, 157
positive 23, 29, 41, 47, 54, 68, 121, 126, 158, 196, 219–222
positive parenting 28
power xiii, 60, 88, 121, 136, 150
praise 36, 154
promise ix, 32, 107
punishment xiv, 28–29

Q
Quick Release 25

R
recycle 112, 157
report, as in abuse or danger 30, 153, 166
respect 9, 29, 33, 46, 50, 58, 87, 89, 98, 122, 133, 150, 154, 157, 176
responsibility xvii, 8, 27, 51, 68, 77, 88, 123, 157
rights xiii, 9, 29, 50, 108, 150, 154, 185, 229

S
sacred space 42, 150
safe 16, 23, 30, 50, 58, 153
safety plan 39, 90–91, 176–

Index

177, 191
Sanskrit 12
school 29, 49, 73, 176,
   194–195, 203–204
self talk 98, 121
shelters 39, 184
Signal for Help 31, 184
solution xvi, 28, 54, 141,
   143, 158, 220–221
Spirit 12, 26, 28, 45, 74,
   100, 135–136, 153, 158,
   161, 188
superpower 22
support 41, 66, 73, 157–158
survivors 39, 183

T

table talk 87
teach 28–29, 32, 36, 38,
   51, 58, 60, 88, 154, 165
technique 22, 189–191
tradition 51, 82, 154, 188
trapped thumb 31. See Signal
   for Help
trauma xvi, 40
treaty 184
triggers 26, 111
trust xi, 28, 47–48, 52, 69,
   83, 88, 90, 96–97, 123,
   139, 150, 170
truth 32, 38, 77, 132, 161

V

vagus nerve 22
video 31, 187–189, 191, 196
violence xiv–xv, 28–29, 39–
   40, 61, 91, 111, 153,
   157–158, 193
   alternatives to violence 61,
      153
volunteer 41, 57, 82, 110,
   198

W

warmline 180
well-being 31, 69, 90, 137
wisdom xvi, 51, 67, 132,
   153
women 39, 132, 185–187,
   191, 201
wonder 14, 84, 96, 100,
   105, 118, 120, 150
write 53–54, 57, 67, 80,
   93, 101, 108, 128, 143,
   217

Y

Youth 27, 49, 57, 202, 204

Also by Debbie Jenae

If Roses Were Blue
Children's adventure story

Your Light, Your Life!
Booklet of pep talks

Be An Inspiration!
First edition of this book

Inspired 101 News
Monthly newsletter

Write On! and *Handwriting @ Work*
More than 300 published handwriting analysis articles

Inspiration Mugs
7 designs each including an inspirational message

Edited and Produced

A Great Flash of Light
Memoir by Frank C. Bognar

Danny Peanuts
Children's story by Gail Boyland

About the Author

Debbie Jenae is an award-winning author, governor's award nominee for outstanding service as a court-appointed child advocate, and founder of Inspired 101. Debbie's fascination and study of behavior and potential includes acupressure, ancient writing, animal symbology, energy medicine, and women's ancient history and influence. She is also Master Certified in Graphoanalysis (handwriting analysis for character and personality) and recipient of the Graphoanalyst of the Year award. From child abuse victim to analyst, author, advocate, speaker, activist, artist, editor, and producer, Debbie is dedicated to increasing understanding, empowering others, and inspiring positive action.

Visit DebbieJenae.com for more.

Important Numbers

In an Emergency   **911**

Poison Control Center   **1-800-222-1222**

Our Phone Number _____

Our Address _____

Hotline _____

Warmline _____

Police _____

Fire _____

Pharmacy _____

School _____

(Name & Number)

Mom _____

Dad _____

Neighbor _____

Doctor _____

Counselor _____

Care Provider _____

Local Friends/Relatives/Other _____

_____

_____

The best way to WOW our world

is to be the *Love* you are.

Don't let anyone dim that light ever!

www.ingramcontent.com/pod-product-compliance
Lightning Source LLC
Chambersburg PA
CBHW051939290426
44110CB00015B/2038